ERICKSONIAN
THERAPY NOW

The Evolution of Psychotherapy

2017   Anaheim
        December 13-17

2017 Evolution Conference special preview edition.

Ericksonian Therapy Now

The Master Class With Jeffrey K. Zeig

with contributions from

Helen Adrienne
Barbara Birge
Grethe Bruun
Caroline Chinlund
Susan Dowell
Bette J. Freedson
Tobi B. Goldfus
Julie Ann Hall
Wei-Kai Hung
Charles M. Iker
Dana Lebo
Rick Miller
Sara Millstein
Susan Pinco
Chanoch Rosenberg
Christoph Sollmann
Robert Staffin
James W. Warnke

and an introduction by

Jeffrey K. Zeig

Zeig, Tucker & Theisen Inc. Publishers
Phoenix, AZ

Layout by Cole Tucker-Walton
Cover Illustration based on a photo by Wei-Kai Hung

Please note that names and identifying characteristics have been changed
throughout this book to protect the privacy of individuals. Any resemblance to a
known person is purely coincidental.

Library of Congress Cataloging-in-Publication Data

Ericksonian Therapy Now:
The Master Class With Jeffrey K. Zeig

/ Zeig, Jeffrey K.—1st edition

p.   cm.

Includes bibliographic references
ISBN 978-1934442-61-6 (pbk : alk paper)

Published by

ZEIG, TUCKER & THEISEN, INC.
2632 East Thomas Rd., Suite 201
Phoenix, AZ 85016
www.zeigtucker.com

Manufactured in the United States of America

Dedicated to Lily Beth

I am one of many who owes a debt to Milton H. Erickson, M.D. His mentorship has been a foundation of my accomplishments in life, both personally and professionally. His signature can be found in the transcripts that follow.

Deep, enduring thanks to my editors, Marnie McGann, who works at the Erickson Foundation, and Suzi Tucker. Suzi and her crew were instrumental in making this book possible.

—Jeff

CONTENTS

Introduction 1
JEFFREY K. ZEIG

1 Listen to Your Own Stories 13
DANA LEBO

Postcard I 29
GRETHE BRUUN

2 Pas De Deux: Utilizing Gestures, Tone, and Pacing to Create Generative Multilevel Communication 31
SUSAN PINCO

3 Experience in a New State: Horsing Around Untethered With Some Friends in Central Park 73
BETTE J. FREEDSON

Postcard II 103
RICK MILLER

4 A Moving Trance 107
CHANOCH ROSENBERG

5 My Stroke, a Stroke of Luck, and My Wise Advisor 125
SUSAN DOWELL

Postcard III 133
SARA MILLSTEIN

6 Traveling Together 135
WEI-KAI HUNG

Postcard IV 155
TOBI B. GOLDFUS

7 On Preparing for Heart Surgery 161
CHRISTOPH SOLLMANN

8 Of Wonder Woman and Super Grannies 169
CAROLINE CHINLUND

Postcard V 187
JULIE ANN HALL

Postcard VI 189
CHARLES M. IKER

9 Take a Line for a Walk 191
JAMES W. WARNKE

Postcard VII 223
BARBARA BIRGE

10 The Utilization of Self in the
Creation of Reference Experiences 225
ROBERT STAFFIN

Epilogue 253
HELEN ADRIENNE

About the Contributors 257

INTRODUCTION

Jeffrey K. Zeig

About This Book

The contributors to this book are indeed the force behind it. Their enthusiasm for the Master Class precipitated the project, and the authors honor me with this book, and in their descriptions of the work we did together. I'm enormously grateful to the contributors, and especially to Helen Adrienne, my co-conspirator. It's a daunting task to do therapy in front of my peers, and it may be even more daunting to publicly disclose my therapy sessions.

It's also quite humbling to see my work in print. Of course, in reading what I have done, I often think of things that I could have done differently. If I'm not careful, this leads to self-criticism. Therefore, as much as possible, I keep in mind my supervision principle of highlighting what is right. Erickson used to say that when we look at a garden, it's just as easy to see the flowers as it is to see the weeds.

I have found it interesting to read the commentaries and understand the meaning that the students project into the work. I'm intentional as a therapist, which means that I work at precisely choosing my words and gestures. Still, just because one intentionally orients toward an effect does not mean that the message sent is the message received and acted upon. Experiential methods are ambiguous and the recipient activates to create meaning. I have a target in mind when I create an experience, but the way it is interpreted depends on the individual.

Over the course of my 40-year career, I have done more public demonstrations than most other experts. My evolution as a therapist has been catalyzed by the Master Classes, in which I have had to invent and reinvent the wheel (or rather, myself).

About the Master Class

"This was the most exquisite training class I have ever taken."
  JW
"These master classes are necessary." HF
"My creativity was spurred in this environment of openness,
  support, and safety." SD
"I feel more empowered and self-assured doing hypnotherapy
  now." JN
"The experiential format facilitated my growth from the inside
  out." DB
"Jeff's artistry is awe inspiring; learning from talented col-
  leagues is joyous." SC
"I am a senior clinician and I keep coming back for more Master
  Classes with Jeff." FJ

These are just some among the testimonials the Master Class has
garnered over the years.

Why has the class inspired such superlatives? How would reading this book provide some of the benefits that have been so obvi-
ously entrancing to participants? It is that the content and the pur-
veyors of that content reflect psychotherapy training at the highest
level. Clinicians who participate in these master classes are not just
seeking training, they are seeking to achieve excellence in themselves on behalf of their clients.

The Master Class consists of actual therapy transcripts with an-
notation from participants. I conducted the demonstration therapies, which were held in a group setting of peers. The problems that
are presented are all from real-life situations. What we are calling
"postcards" are peppered throughout the text offering brief impres-
sions—anxiety about first-time participation, the joy of forging life-
long friendships, and some of my strengths and foibles.

This book is an opportunity to study single session therapies
that are based in experiential methods. The learning from these
methods is primarily stimulated by the client living the change, not

by intellectual understanding of how to change. The participants declare what they are going to do differently and the sessions are designed to create experiences that foster the accomplishment of stated goals. Participants have solved complex problems and have made significant life changes. They have overcome writer's block and then completed a book; they are happier in their jobs and relationships; they rebalance work and life; and they surmount childhood trauma.

This book will not only solidify learning for past and current Master Class attendees but will also benefit those who have not attended. The contributors to the book are all experienced clinicians and instructors of psychotherapy who have attended multiple classes, in some cases more than 30 meetings. It is an honor to lead these classes. I have learned so much. I have grown so much.

The Structure of the Master Class

The Master Class is limited to 12 experienced clinicians who assemble for a four-day training course held Thursday to Sunday for approximately seven hours each day.

Over the four days, each attendee assumes four roles: a demonstration patient with me; a patient with a peer; one role as supervisor for a therapist/patient pair; and one as a therapist for a peer. I supervise both the therapists and supervisors.

Each day consists of two types of structures with a total of six sessions per day alternating between the demonstrations that I conduct with a patient/participant and the ones in which three participants work in the roles of therapist, patient, and supervisor. In the first hour, I offer the demonstration therapy with one of the students. The next structure is a triad, with one peer therapist, one client, and one peer supervisor. I serve as meta-supervisor. The two types of structures are alternated throughout the day. Three are held before lunch, three after lunch.

When I am the therapist, the structure lasts for approximately 50 minutes, leaving time for a short break before the next. Student therapies are designed to last a maximum of 45 minutes, allowing time for supervision and a break. However, the time parameters are flexible; some will run longer than others.

The environment in the class is intimate and supportive and the learning experience is rich and fertile. Although focused on experiential approaches derived from the work of Milton Erickson, this program provides an opportunity to advance clinical skills regardless of professional orientation and level of experience. Each student's learning experience is tailored to focus on his or her orientation. If the student is interested in becoming a better cognitive behavioral therapist, the supervision is designed to provide that experience.

Setting

The classes are held in the office of the host, Helen Adrienne. Her office is located on New York City's upper east side. Students sit on chairs and couches in a space that is big enough to comfortably hold a dozen people. Two armchairs near the window are reserved for the therapy sessions that are set up to be filmed. Although dulcet tones can provide the most adaptive experience for a client, in this class it is important that all the students adequately hear what is happening in the session. Therefore, personal amplifiers are used for the therapist and client.

Procedures

On the first day, the students meet at 8:30 AM to establish the time slots in which each person can expect to work in each role, and to clarify administrative considerations, expectations, and protocols for supervision. We meet at 9 AM the rest of the time.

Supervision

Supervision occurs after the sessions in which a participant is the therapist. The supervision can be active or passive. If the therapist requests active supervision, then either the supervisor or I can interrupt the session. If the supervision is passive, neither the supervisor nor I will interject unless the therapist requests support. Because of time constraints there are no opportunities for general discussion among students regarding the individual therapy sessions.

After the supervision, I supervise the supervisor and provide feedback to the therapist. In recent years, Helen Adrienne has joined me as a co-supervisor. Helen's supervision tends to be more experiential and mine more didactic, and it's proven a good combination for the attendees.

The supervisor's job is to provide feedback to the therapist by indicating four or five things that the therapist did effectively, and then two or three things that the therapist could do differently next time. In the history of the master classes in New York City only one person was ever criticized and that was for being blatantly disrespectful to the client.

Feedback

Students receive the following instruction about feedback prior to coming to the class:

Supervision feedback is solution focused. In general, there is one rule in providing the feedback to a therapist in the Master Class—do not criticize! No criticism or negative comments should be offered, unless the therapist seriously breaches ethical standards. Feedback should be positive, concrete, and geared toward possibilities for change. Feedback provided by supervisors should consist of:

1. At least three specific things the therapist did well plus concrete examples illustrating each point. Take copious notes if necessary.
2. At least one other option for the therapist to consider in the future.

Please remember, no criticism in this class. This ensures a safe environment where all can grow.

Videotaping

We provide videotaping so that attendees can review the sessions afterward. The video recording is for personal use only and will not be utilized or stored. If students do not want their sessions to be videotaped, which is fine, they can let us know. We assume everyone wants to be videotaped, unless a participant requests otherwise. If group members provide permission, attendees can have access to all sessions. For a limited time, the files are placed on Dropbox. These files are confidential for attendees only and are NOT to be shared.

Goals

Specifying goals in each area has been key in the success of the Master Class. When the class was first initiated, goals were written on large pieces of paper and posted around the room. Now they are written on a handout provided prior to the class.

Since each person participates in four roles, to have maximum benefit, that person must have personal development goals for each role. Goals for personal issues for when the participant is the patient are set in advance of class so that students will not be rushed into deciding on a goal before taking an active role.

The following information is sent to students prior to the class. Participants prepare their answers prior to attending.

1. Therapist role:

Take a moment and think about yourself as a therapist. Think about your personal strengths and the areas in which you seek improvement. What do you want to develop in yourself as a therapist? What is your professional development goal? What is your growing edge as a therapist? How can you use your time at this Master Class to improve and become a better professional?

Please write three specific self-development goals. Keep in mind that you may gain clarity as the program progresses, in which case you can amend your goals.

2. Client with Dr. Zeig and with a peer:

What goals do I have? Where am I stuck in moving forward? What is currently bothering me? What are my patterns carried over from childhood that interfere with present life? Has past trauma played a part in my life's narrative or current problems? Do I have any bad habits that I'd like to overcome? How can I improve in my relationships and/or in my marriage? How can I resolve blocks to personal achievement?

3. Supervisor for a peer:

What is your goal as a supervisor? Perhaps you are not a supervisor, and have never supervised. (If so, that's okay. Just think about how you would like to be if you were in a supervisor position.) What has helped you in past supervisions? Think about what you would like to develop in yourself. Perhaps as a supervisor you'd like to be experiential, use metaphors, discern interaction patterns, develop better utilization skills, etc.

Please write three specific goals.

The History of the Master Class

The first Master Class was held in New York City in May of 2002. It was initiated by Helen Adrienne, who had attended the advanced didactic training program held in Phoenix, Arizona, under the auspices of The Milton H. Erickson Foundation. Helen contacted me about other training possibilities and I told her that if she could bring together a dozen students, we could create a Master Class. Helen immediately jumped into action and found interested colleagues. During the early years, we held four master classes per year, one each quarter. Eventually, however, we dropped the summer class and now classes are held winter, spring, and fall.

The Master Classes fill up quickly. Currently, there is already a two-year waiting list. Attendees of the Master Class must be licensed to practice in the health/mental health fields in the region in which they live. Students travel from all over the United States, as well as from many different countries, including Germany, France, Denmark, Greenland, and Taiwan. All classes are held in English. Many students are immersed in Ericksonian therapy; however, an interest in this is not required. Some of the students are renowned teachers of psychotherapy.

Since the inception of the New York Master Class, I have conducted 52 classes in New York City alone. I lead master classes in other countries such as Austria, Belgium, China, France, Germany, Mexico, Singapore, Taiwan, and Turkey. Because each class is unique, most students return to participate in additional classes. Helen Adrienne has attended all 52 New York Master Classes, and she is followed closely by another participant who has attended 50 classes! Most sign on for multiple classes, but we do try to hold open some spaces for new students.

One of the reasons that the Master Classes have been so successful is the group dynamic. The students quickly bond. They eat meals together, they partner with others to tour the city, and in doing this they create a community from which growth emerges. The attendees have knowledge in different arenas, and their diversity make the class a richer experience. Most important has been the expectation that focus will be on what the participant does well and what he or she can look forward to doing even better, ensuring a sense of safety and acceptance.

There's an antecedent to the Master Class that I would like to acknowledge. In 1973, shortly after earning my master's degree in clinical psychology from San Francisco State University, I attended a one-year training program in transactional analysis and group therapy led by Bob and Mary Goulding. My supervision in the Master Class mirrors this couple's model. The Gouldings were

extraordinary practitioners and their focus was experiential realization. I admired how public they were with their work. Perhaps I unconsciously decided that one day I would be just as open with mine.

Milton Erickson, who I also met in 1973, was my mentor in-
termittently for more than six years; he was also an inspiration in
creating the Master Class. At his essence, Erickson was experiential.
He was the most radically experiential therapist to ever practice. I
don't think it's hyperbole to state that Erickson was experiential
more than 90 percent of the time. His experiential methods included using hypnosis, tasks, and anecdotes. Creating transformative
experiences is a component in many schools of therapy, including
rational emotive behavior therapy and cognitive behavior therapy,
but for Erickson being experiential was not merely a component;
it was most of his therapeutic work. Hypnosis is essentially an experiential technique. The subtext of hypnosis is this: "By living this
experience, you can be different." Hypnosis is not a means of providing information.

The Focus of the Master Class

The Master Class is a unique opportunity for therapist growth and
development. It is centered on learning how to be a better therapist. Most workshops teach participants how to do therapy, which
can be learned by instruction or by reading theory, technique, and
research. But how to be a therapist requires personal development
through direct supervision and having direct experience with effective therapy.

Regardless of their theoretical orientation, students are encouraged to be experiential. Central to this idea is a therapist using his
or her entire palette to be more effective. The Master Classes are
designed to expand the therapist's palette. Traditional methods that
are central to effective psychotherapy can be made experiential to
increase impact.

For instance, most therapists primarily use verbal communication in their work. But the spectrum of communication is much

broader and can include using the microdynamic level—tone, tempo, pauses in speech, prosody, and proximity. In reading Erickson, one realizes that he explored how nuances found in the vast range of communication possibilities could be used effectively. Therapists are free to enhance typical verbal communication with gestures and sounds, or the use of random props found around the room.

An underlying philosophy is that all clients have resources that may not be immediately available. Every smoker knows how to be comfortable without a cigarette. Every anxious client knows how to relax. The job of the therapist in each session is to utilize whatever is available in the complex weave of the client's life and to harness those things experientially to promote change.

Among the elements that have been explored in previous Master Classes:

- Being experiential
- Looking for interactional solutions
- Bringing the problem into the present moment
- Making therapy a visual experience, especially by using gestures and paraverbal communication
- Being ironic about the problem, not about the client
- Utilizing context, including objects in the room
- Getting out of the therapist's chair, making therapy a drama of change
- Sculpting a problem or solution state
- Using anecdotes
- Tailoring
- Being strategic
- Using seeding
- Attunement as the social basis of empathy
- Finding a theme and returning to it to create cohesiveness
- Making therapy an artistic improvisation
- Using metaphor
- Using sound effects
- Being intentional

- Being precise
- Being systemic
- The strategic use of insight
- The strategic use of questions

You are invited to look for these elements in the transcripts included in The Master Class!

CHAPTER ONE

Listen to Your Own Stories

Dana Lebo

The Setting

Dana, a 50-something psychologist from North Carolina, takes her seat opposite Dr. Jeff Zeig, who calmly waits for her to settle into her patient role. In contrast to Jeff, Dana is fidgety. She attempts to position earphones and a microphone around her head, fumbling with the straps, tangling her hair in the wires, and placing the earphones upside down. Jeff patiently helps her adjust the headset, points to the on-switch, and once the tiny green light appears on the battery box, Dana relaxes back into her chair, testing the volume.

"Can you hear me okay?" she croaks, startling the 11 other clinicians—some who have travelled from as close as midtown Manhattan and others from as far away as Germany—into attention mode. Sue, one of the observing therapists, checks the video camera to make sure it is rolling. She gives Dana and Jeff a thumbs up. So far, so good.

J: Notes? (*Jeff looks at the scribble-filled pad on Dana's lap.*)

D: Yep. (*Dana nods.*) I got my notes. (*She waves her pad in the air.*) I haven't really said hello to you yet. Hello!

J: Welcome! (*Jeff smiles.*)

D: It's great to be here, and thank you for putting me on the first day.

Dana points to the schedule on the far wall of the room that lists the roles and assignments of the 12 therapists attending the Master Class. The schedule covers half the wall—four days, six sessions a day. The structure of the schedule is unique. Each therapist rotates among the roles of patient, therapist, and supervisor over the four days. Dana can see her name near the top of the schedule next to Jeff's. She is listed as his afternoon patient on Day One of the Class.

D: I know it's true I have a trend of being last. I don't know how that happens. I somehow get plunked into that last spot (*she eyes the final sessions on the schedule where her name usually appears, shakes her head, and gives a helpless shrug*). But, quite honestly, I actually enjoy being last (*her voice takes on a tone of discovery*). Because I think there's a wonderful evolution that occurs throughout the four days here. We go through 12 therapies with each person who sits in this chair. (*Dana pats the arms of her chair for emphasis.*) So always by the end I feel I've been cured 12 times over and I've got nothing to talk about and so (*her face reflects appreciation*) I can just sit here and let you work your magic and help me connect the dots with whatever just happens to pop into my head.

J: Good summary. (*Jeff nods.*)

D: And you're good at that. The skill that I admire—among many that I admire in you—is that ability to just pick out the dots and help to lay them out there for us to connect. (*While talking, Dana points to imaginary dots in the air in front of her, and then connects them with a sweep of her hand.*) And one of the things that I like to do before sitting in this chair is go to the river (*referring to the Harlem River on the East side of Manhattan, just a couple of blocks from where the Master Class is located*) because I never know what I'm going to talk about, or what my challenges or problems and opportunities are. I never have the luxury of just being able to talk about them. So I go to the river and just sit there for a few minutes. (*She ponders for a moment.*) What's that phrase? Let the river run through me? (*She nods to herself, remembering the movie with a similar title and an image of Brad Pitt, pants and shirtsleeves rolled up, fly fishing in the middle of the coursing river, casting his line into the water with masterful skill and grace, at one with the nature of it all.*) Just let go and then it comes to me. And then I tell you and just plop it out and then you come up with something.

J: Plop away and see what I come up with. (*Jeff's tone is playful, inviting Dana to continue.*)

The Problem:
The Swelling, the La Brea Tar Pit Couch, and the Bad Funk

D: So, as I was saying before, I think there's a piece from all the therapies that we can absorb and find some use in our own lives, and I'm sorry that Harriet left (*Dana looks at the couch where Harriet, a therapist who is known for her prolific writing, had been sitting earlier that day*) because I thank her for bringing up that writing theme, which has already come up more than once today. And the piece that I got from it was how lately, these last couple of months, I've been feeling this tremendous swelling inside of me (*Dana clasps her hands over her chest*), this swelling in the sense of—kind of this—I don't know (*she struggles to find the right words, and her voice rises in intensity*) …this urge, this push, this kind of voracious desire or appetite to write.

The time has come (*she says rather firmly*) just to sit down and let go without even knowing what I'm going to write about, and I am just wanting to do that badly. And then, well… (*her voice trails off as she remembers all that gets in the way*) …having the normal routine of get up in the morning and do my triathlon training… (*Dana's tone changes to resignation as she describes her daily regimen that includes everything but writing*) …and go to my work and put my all into a full day and then come home and play chauffeur and get the kids to their various activities and make dinner and be part of the family life at nighttime (*she sighs deeply*). As much as I can muster up any energy I have left at that point, I sit down on the couch every night, thinking now's my time. I'm gonna just let that swell come out and I'm gonna just let… (*Dana stretches her arms out in front of her, curving her hands as if she is about to tap away on a keyboard, but her fingers remain motionless.)*

Like Jim here *(she nods her head towards Father Jim),* I suspend my arms to see what will flow out of my fingertips—and guess what happens? *(She pauses, as if she is waiting for someone to answer for her, but the room is silent.)* I fall asleep! Every night I get to that point, laptop right there, ready to perform, and *(her voice fills with indignation)* I fall asleep!

Dana continues to describe her problem of falling asleep, or getting sucked into the depths of the "La Brea Tar Pit Couch" (as her husband calls it), while her kids gleefully stick stuffed animals in the crooks of her arms, draw mustaches on her face, and take pictures of her drooling on the pillow to share with their friends on Snapchat.

Stories of Swelling

No matter how many nights she has succumbed to the La Brea Tar Pit Couch, Dana tells Jeff that the swelling is still there.

She then shares with Jeff several stories about how she has experienced the sense of swelling in her life, assuring him in the process that "I'm sure all of this circles back together somehow." To emphasize the promise of "circling back," she pats a spiral-shaped pendant she is wearing from New Zealand. Although at the time Dana is uncertain about the symbolism of her pendant, she feels that on some level, the spiral must depict her felt sense of a force swelling and expanding from within and then circling back to the point from which it started. Sure enough, at a later date, a quick Google search confirms her intuition about the pendant's meaning. The Maori people of New Zealand called it "koru," the word for "loop," based on the shape of an unfurling silver fern frond: "Its circle conveying perpetual movement and its inner coil suggesting a return to the point of origin"—according to an undisputed Wikipedia source.

Through each story, Dana describes her experiences and nuances of "swelling." To swim through the swells of the sea in New Zealand, she was advised not to resist, but instead, to allow the waves to carry her. To help her go with the flow, she sang "Weee!" at the crest of each swell. At a fiber arts store, she listened for her favorite work of art to call out to her, like a voice beckoning her to pay attention, to take notice. "That calling is like the swelling," she explains. "It's like the calling for me to write and I hear it." And in the process of writing, she felt a force swelling within her. She described the same feeling when, in college, she would lose herself in painting into the wee hours of the morning. What she wants more than anything is for Jeff to somehow help her to transform any negative "funks" she experiences that stand in the way of writing into the more positive feeling of lightness associated with swelling. Still, she has to be careful, she explains. If she were too swept away by the moments of swelling and creative expression, if she were too absorbed in those time warps, she could forget the day-to-day demands of motherhood—leaving her kids stranded in a dark, empty parking lot after swimming or soccer practice, a sink of dirty dishes, and no supper waiting for them at home.

J: Okay.

Dana continues to describe how for years she avoided the dangers of the time warps.

D: I had to put the paintings aside, literally… down in the basement. Old paintings… just there to remind me. Now is not the time to be a painter. And there was a 6-month period before I started my new job in North Caroline and I took those paintings out and I took a couple canvases and I cut them up and I re-sewed them back together and it was tremendously gratifying. I didn't finish but I started and it just felt so good to rework what I had painted years ago into fiber art.

On some level, Dana finds herself, like the Maori loop in her necklace, referring to her own cycles of creative expansion and circling back to the point where they began. She gives Jeff a questioning look.

D: So now to circle back. Can I apply that same feeling to the bad funks? …If I can just have that openness in those moments of bad funk and those seizures that seize creativity. If I can just be creative in those moments instead of make them worse.

J: So far so good. And the writing. What does your heart dictate? What do you want to write?

D: Well, it is still like a canvas…

J: It is a quilt.

D: Yeah.

J: And so if you just make a patch, then how the quilt will come together, will eventually come to you.

D: (*Nods her head in agreement.*) And I know if I just start quilting, it will come. Of course, certainly, outlines help and all that. But I always deviate from the outline.

Jeff looks thoughtful.

J: Gregory Bateson used to tell a story. It was the earlier days of computers and so this is an apocryphal story. Not true.

And so an expert who had invented computers decided he was going to invent artificial intelligence. So he got the greatest minds together to create a computer that would really do artificial intelligence and after some period of time they thought they had gotten the algorithm that they had created the computer with artificial intelligence. And so they typed the question, "Do you have the intelligence of a human being?" into the computer. So this daisy wheel printer starts to spin….and the answer comes out onto the paper. And they rush over there to the paper to look at what the answer is and what is typed on the paper from the computer is, "That reminds me of a story."

Jeff smiles and everyone laughs. Dana, however, looks a bit confused. She's uncertain how Jeff's apocryphal story applies to her real ones. Later, months after the session is over, she will look up Bateson's story on the Internet, hoping more information will clear her confusion.

She finds the original source of the computer joke in the book, Angels Fear, which Bateson's daughter, Mary, coauthored with her father. In the chapter, "Metalogue: Why Do You Tell Stories?" Mary asks her father why he "tells the same stories again and again." Dana gasps as she reads Bateson's response to his daughter's question, wondering if Jeff has any idea about an incredible coincidence. That is, after Bateson tells Mary the computer joke, he asks her to give him "that conch over there" on the mantelpiece, and explains, "Now, what we have here is a whole set of different stories, very beautiful stories indeed... This conch is what's called a right-handed spiral, and spirals are sort of pretty things too— that shape which can be increased in one direction without altering its basic proportions. So the shell has the narrative of its individual growth pickled within its geometric form as well as the story of its evolution... And then, you see, even though the conch has protrusions that keep it from rolling around the ocean floor, it's been worn and abraded, so that's still another story."

Months after her session, Dana was still discovering some powerful symbols between the lines of her own stories and the one that Jeff shared. First the Maori spiral, then the Conch's spiral shell which for hundreds of years was used to signify truth and light, attract positive energy, protect from negative energy and communicate the sound OMMMMM – maybe, through connecting all the dots, Dana was beginning to see a cure for the negative funk after all!

Jeff's Technique—
One Small Thing You Would Do Differently

Jeff continues to explain.

J: So the swelling is to write the stories. Now if you allow yourself into the La Brea Tar Pits then your physiological tiredness seizes you and grips you and suddenly you are in a different kind of funk because you're not meeting the dictates of what you want to do with that feeling. Okay, so now what would you do different? What's one—coach yourself—tell me one little thing you would do different... with regard to when you feel that swelling and you have time to write, what would you do different? If you feel that you are starting to enter into somebody else's funk, what's one thing that you do different? (*He accentuates his request for one thing different by pulling his right hand towards himself.*)

D: Well, when I feel that pull into... (*Dana mirrors Jeff's movement with a pull of her own hand*) ...well, if we're talking about somebody else's funk, take a deep breath and say, Oh isn't it fascinating how I am being sucked into this tar pit of depression and despair and negativity and crap.

J: So, oh, isn't it interesting? (*Jeff models the question for Dana.*)

D: So, isn't it interesting? (*She repeats.*)

J: So, that is a balancing moment. Oh, isn't it interesting? And that gives you a moment to reflect on which path it is you can choose to take when you hear Oh, isn't that interesting? When you feel that swelling.

D: (*Dana nods.*) And I also ask, So what evolutionary purpose does this negative funk have? Is there something in there I can pull from this that's constructive?

Like anger is a signal that there is something unjust in the situation? Or things are out of control? Or someone has slighted me in some way or you know I feel manipulated or used or that kind of thing. So, anger is a signal to speak up. So what is someone else's funk? I mean we are talking about two funks here. We are talking about the funk of being sucked into someone else's negative funk. And we are also talking about the funk of sitting on the couch.

J: (*Jeff rests his face on his fist, nodding as Dana is speaking.*) Or getting into your own negative funk.

D: Right. Which, well, I'm asleep. I'm not into anything.

J: Do something with me. And make yourself comfortable. (*Jeff leans forward, moving to the edge of his seat, and places his hands palms upward.*) Put yourself… Get rid of—

D: —the notes. (*Dana puts her pad on the floor beside her, and hoists herself forward, facing Jeff head-on.*)

The Trance

J: And then as you orient comfortably, just allow yourself to sit back and take an easy breath. Perhaps put your elbows down at your side—if that takes any pressure off your shoulders. (*Jeff models sitting comfortably in the chair, back straight, elbows by his side, hands on his knees, while Dana adjusts her own position to match his.*) And then you effortlessly orient to me and you can use me as a focal point for a moment and then gradually begin to recognize that as you orient to me that you can begin to slow down, for example, your breathing. That for example the periphery of your vision may become grey or blurry. That you can notice a tendency to want to allow your eyes to just blink, to shut on you so you can further enjoy going inside and learn something about the story of your own trance and begin to gradually and effortlessly…

And then you know how you can play back that sporting event and you can play back that sporting event as a replay and you can play and replay what it is that you've experienced. And so in the privacy of your mind, I'd like you to replay the story of New Zealand and the way in which you can feel intimidated and the way in which you can feel overwhelmed by the environment and the way in which it seems as if there was threatening or uncomplimentary weather or weather which couldn't complement your journey, and the way in which somebody could come up to you and recognizing some of the circumstances that you were in, could say to you just go with the swells and realize that you could just allow yourself to float, relax, enjoy, enjoy the swells and let them guide you and let them take you to a place where you continue your journey and the emotion, the heartfelt emotion that you experienced. As if that moment of some-one coming up to you is a defining moment and that you can really absorb that defining moment in such a way that you understand and you hold into your heart those words, just go with the swells, and that the essence of your own understanding, of seeing the fiber art in the way that you could see the fiber art and recognizing intuitively what calls you and how you move effortlessly because this is what calls you. And the recognition of taking some canvasses and patching them together, and the curious nature of the way in which even though there's the inexorable force of gravity that seems to pull you down that there's a way in which you hold yourself in an upright posture effortlessly and you don't need to think about that. There's a sense of balance in the muscles of your neck and shoulders that allows you to hold yourself in that upright posture even though that seemingly inexorable force is there all around you. And hearing and listening and playing and replaying those stories so that you can extract from those stories something that really is essential to you that becomes you that are defining moments. And so for a moment you can be reliving New Zealand that you can be reliving a moment in which you move yourself out of that funk and for a moment you can be reliving your art so that you can really understand so that you can realize the power of your own stories to guide you and taking this meditative moment in trance to really understand, to really feel what it is that you said.

To grasp the importance of what you said, to grasp the guidance of your own stories. And Dana, what is it that you're doing now, where are you now with your story? (*Jeff pauses for Dana to respond.*)

D: Uh, well. Kind of riding the waves...

Dana describes to Jeff a high school memory—seeing the movie Helen Keller *in English class, and the "aha" moment when Helen made the connection between seeing and hearing. Days later, Dana's English teacher read to the class an essay in which a classmate described that special moment of awareness. Dana didn't even realize until the end that the essay her teacher had read was not another classmate's, but her own. Even then, Dana had experienced that feeling of the swell and a force moving through her. Years later, her son Jacob, then 5 years old, gave her a birthday card on which he drew a roller coaster with "swells" and underneath, the words: Let's have fun on your birthday. We!!!!!*

Dana draws the curves of her son's roller coaster in the air—as if she were conducting an orchestra.

D: And I have that card on my bulletin board at work and I look at it everyday (*she shares from her state of trance*).

J: So that you can further reinforce the "we" experience and so that feeling, that swelling feeling is really there and if you accompany it as it accompanies you and in this reflective moment, this moment of quiet that we call trance you are able to further instill inside of yourself the realization of that feeling and the importance of the words, the words you are saying and the meaning that those words have to you in your heart and the way in which the story has a synergy that's more than any of the sum of its parts. And it's nice to just take time to realize the import of your words, to realize the power of your words, to realize the power of your story so that you confidently impress upon yourself the realizations that are contained therein.

And where does that take you now?

D: I guess I'm feeling the power of a moment of sadness. I am remembering a moment when Jeremy, my son, was mad at Ingrid, our exchange student... He said something so mean to Ingrid she started crying and there was so much anguish in her face and her eyes were just like the eyes of a little child lost and hurt and I said, "Jeremy look at Ingrid." He was so busy in his own anger and he looked at her and said, "Holy shit, did I do that?" And he was transformed. That angry mean boy was transformed. One look at her anguish. He went over and he hugged her. And I left the room and when I came back they were laughing and talking and later Ingrid came up to me and said, "Thank you. We're better than ever now." And she said, "I didn't know how useful my crying was... Wow, look what happened when I cry." That moment. That transformative moment.

J: And the way in which you work can suddenly emerge as a really transformative moment. And what I'm inviting you to do at this moment is to reflect on your stories and to feel the transformative power of your words in a way that you didn't before and that I can hear the transformative power of your stories and the words of your stories and that I'm inviting you to identify with those stories and that I'm inviting you to hear the elements of those stories and I'm inviting you to hear the transformative power of those words in such a way that they become you, in such a way that they incorporate them in such a way that you breathe them in and you view and review them and play and replay them so that you can distill for yourself the empowerment that they represent. And where does that leave you now?

D: What you just described feels like the cycle on here. (*Dana points to her Maori swirl necklace.*)

J: Closing the loop.

D: (*Dana nods, continuing to point to the center of her pendant.*) Closing the loop and at the center is the moment that I can write it. It is the right moment to write. It is just when it comes out.

After repeating it. After saying the story again and after distilling it down and feeling the felt sense of those moments of power. That's the center of this. That's the moment to write.

J: Okay, so, hold onto that. Intensify. Feel your grip on that. Take it in. And there's a certain pride that can begin to come up out in the realization of realizing the center. Your center.

And then when you're ready I invite you to bring yourself back here. So that you can take one or two or three easy breaths and begin to reorient and bring yourself back.

And then gradually open your eyes. And so what's the take-away?

D: Good question. (*Dana pauses to think for a moment.*) It's the, there's a confidence, that the moment will come.

J: Okay.

D: And at the same time, I've got to set the stage for it.

J: Okay, you get to set the stage for it.

D: I get to set the stage for it.

J: Uh huh.

D: And it may not happen next weekend. And it may not happen next month. But it will come.

J: And your confidence in that.

D: It's a sad confidence.

J: What's the sadness?

D: That it may not come for even a year and I don't want it to be that far away.

J: There's a lot of responsibilities and a lot of people and a lot of things that call you and interpose between that swelling sensation.

D: I guess there's a takeaway in the aha moment, the realization that every day is full of stories and while I am patiently confident that day will come that I can sit down and it will fall out of me, everyday stories happen, and if I can just be in those stories and allow the force to take them in and play them and play them again and distill them down—I am writing everyday even though the words aren't yet on paper.

J: And if I may be more blunt with you and more direct and suggest the takeaway is to listen to your stories. To hear your stories. To feel what your stories are saying to you. And to incorporate the message of what your stories are saying. And my takeaway for you is that somehow you've been ignoring the essence of your own stories. You work in a coaching situation so you have a coaching mentality. You can tease that out, you can play with that. And if it means something, you can reflect on that and realize more fully what you've been saying. I don't know where else to take that with you right now. I just want to clarify what could be a takeaway.

D: Um hum, that's a great takeaway.

And I'm going to listen again and again and again.

J: Listen how?

D: To the tape, and...

J: Don't listen to me. Listen to you. I'd be interested to hear what happens when you do that.

Two Years Later

"Listen to your own stories." That was the advice Jeff Zeig had given when I asked him to help me out of a negative funk. Now here I am, two years later, feeling that same funk—the downward pull, the vegetable mind, the shortfall of energy no matter how hard I try to bounce back to a perkier state. I am once again fascinated with my ability to just sink into the couch and allow the Le Brea Tar Pits to suck me in. Stuck again.

At first, I was confused at how he had arrived at the advice, "Listen to your own stories," when I was hoping he could just instill in me some kind of switch that I could flip on when the funk arrived and I needed a lift. But listening to the tape of our conversation, I realized I was sharing story after story after story; after all, I had been "storying" up for a year since my last visit to the Master Class.

One story was about Ingrid, our exchange student from Norway who had to resort to tears to make my angry teenage son finally hear what she was saying. Another story was about the triathlon from hell in New Zealand. After traveling halfway around the world to compete, I was met by gale force winds, ocean swells, and torrential downpours—barely could I propel myself forward on land, in air, or sea. I also told a story about cutting up the canvases I had painted in my early 20s so I could sew them back together as fiber art in midlife.

They were funny, quirky, scattered stories. If I tried to draw from them a common theme, all I could summon was—well, how about transformation? Ingrid, in a moment of anguish and tears, caused her host brother to transform his mood from indignant anger to compassion. A triathlete from California, who was used to swimming in stormy waters advised me to ride the waves like a roller coaster, singing "weeeee!" in my head, turning my anxiety into excitement. My fiber art, although yet unfinished, was an attempt to rework, unknot, and reform my 20-something's creations into a new type of canvas that was more expressive of my 40-something me.

It didn't hit me until I revisited them two years later, and saw myself on tape staring blankly at Jeff as he repeated his simple advice: "Listen to your stories." Bubbling from within, my stories contained the truth about how to dunk the funk. To transform my mood, like Dorothy in *The Wizard of Oz*, all I had to do was listen to myself.

What stories do I have to share today? In June, my son Alex, our Golden Boy Alex, was diagnosed with pediatric cancer. Last October, I experienced my daughter Sandra give birth to her own daughter, Ryan Rose. Jeremy, my senior in high school, spent the Twelve Days of Christmas applying to twelve colleges. And Jacob, our youngest, is asking for the car keys. As I write these sentences, I feel the stories brewing inside me, and the full range of moods from untold denial, anger, and sadness to peace, joy, and transcendence stirring within. Just listen to my stories. Give them a voice. Hear what they have to say. Allow the words to swell up and write them down.

As I sit right now on my Le Brea Tar Pit couch, wide awake, fingers dancing on the keyboard, I think of Jeff and the Master Class in New York and their impact. And the words and songs come from somewhere, from a place that is springy, playful, and free. To dunk the funk, all I have to do is open the trunk, throw out the junk, hug the hunk, dance with the punk, meditate like a monk, and no matter how far I've sunk, climb back to the top bunk. And at the peak of each swell, sing weeeeee!!!

Ignition:
A Turning Point in a New York City Flat

Grethe Bruun

The feeling flowing through my body is sudden—here I am in New York City boasting about my work in Denmark. When I say it, I am met with hearty laughter from the Master Class that comforts me, and this mood of permission helps me carry on when Jeff smiles at me and asks me more questions. Sentence by sentence the story develops, and he plays the role of a midwife helping the development of a rich story of my professional life—spoken for the first time with pride and happiness while being met by curiosity and an eagerness to know more, which supports me surprisingly to go on and on...

My presupposition was that I would be invited into deep trance by the great master, and here I was sitting and having an equal conversation with him, and he "just" continued to ask questions. Gradually I began to enjoy sharing my heart matters in my work and had a bodily feeling of owning what I was sharing.

Afterwards it dawned on me that this is a royal example of tailoring in supervision: allowing me to do "some big talking," mirroring the working reality and updating my internal professional story.

On my way back to Denmark, I became aware of a meta message, which ignited the following new belief: If you can talk like that about your work with a high-ranking psychologist, you can evolve your work further.

As my primary focus as a psychologist is supervision, I went back and added a masterclass of supervision for psychologists to my working area. I now lead two masterclasses, each meeting six days a year. Every second year I meet with Jeff about my work in the masterclass and those meetings always spark many new daring thoughts and actions for me, supported by the belief that you can always do more. One time I told Jeff that I felt I had been bold and his reply was: "You can be even bolder!" This remark triggered a lot of brain activity. Since I joined the master class the first time, I have written a book on hypnosis in therapy and in supervision, have made speeches at conferences, and am leading an ongoing hypnosis group... all in co-creation with and support from supervisees and colleagues. I also co-supervised a master class with Jeff in Denmark.

The Master Class in New York has been like a playground for me in which I get to meet other playmates and cultures, and play in a language that is not my native tongue. I have felt very respected and free.

In my mind, Jeff has gone from being an unreachable Master to a real person walking around the apartment in his socks ready to meet me. Simultaneously, I acknowledge his great know-how and knowledge in hypnosis, and most of all I appreciate our human encounter in our conversations, always looking forward to where our next conversation will take me.

CHAPTER TWO

Pas De Deux:
Utilizing Gestures, Tone, and Pacing to Create Generative Multilevel Communication

Susan Pinco

The master class with Jeff Zeig is one of the highlights of my year. There is something indescribably delicious about coming together with 12 skilled therapists poised to take another leap in their evolution. Remarkably, and counter to what one would expect in group development, the group welcomes and absorbs new members so rapidly that it almost defies imagination. In fact, people become cherished members almost before we all know their names. This is a true testament to the loving and supportive atmosphere that Jeff and Helen Adrienne, our host and co-teacher, create.

While we no longer put up poster sized papers listing our goals as therapist, supervisor, and patient, we are nonetheless encouraged to envision these goals and to articulate them at the beginning of our work sessions. Within this structure we, in our therapist roles, are encouraged to think strategically and, if possible, create a symphony with a discernible beginning, middle, and end replete with theme, melody, and chorus. As I am still striving to do this, I find that I appreciate more and more of Jeff's artistry each time I watch him work. It never ceases to amaze me how he can teach on so many levels in his roles as therapist, supervisor, mentor, and friend. Stepping outside the traditional confines of these roles, Jeff, masterfully crafts our experience in a way that excites the creative spark in all of us, nurturing the seeds of our next blossoming.

I've chosen the session from our January 2014 class to illustrate how Jeff utilizes gestures, tone, and pacing to add dimension and texture to his work, which is both simple and extraordinarily complex. In it he elegantly unpacks the issues I am struggling with in a way that allows me to embody both the problem and the solution.

As you read this transcript I invite you to notice Jeff's use of himself, the way he keeps me from getting lost in the forest of details that I am sometimes drawn into, and the way that he anchors, and vivifies, the work with movement and metaphor.

Jeff: Okay, What is the intended destination?	This is said with eyes sparking, a playful lilt to his voice, and a gesture with his arms that is a combination of welcoming, embracing, and expansive. As he speaks he emphasizes both "intended" and "destination."
S: Oh God...um...more ease...	I respond with a similar gesture and these words. My body demonstrates that this is clearly a desirable goal and that I am half way there as I am sitting with an open posture with my arms resting on the arms of the chair, while my legs are folded tightly around the legs of the chair like a pretzel.
and the thing that I've been struggling with is my reaction to lies...	Jeff responds with a brief nod as I continue, his body is a relaxed reflection of mine, with his legs crossed and missing the tension found in mine. And we are off and running.

Jeff: Uh-huh...	More nods, eyes riveted on my face, and his mouth slightly open amplifying his rapt attention.

I tell a bit of my story which relates to my newly acquired responsibilities related to my aging parents, who are in their 90s, and who until very recently, have been active, independent, and vital. They have both sharply declined in the past 10 months. My father, age 94, has had numerous hospitalizations for TIAs (mini strokes), and injuries from falls. Following the last hospitalization my father reluctantly agreed to stop driving. My mother wisely stopped driving a number of years earlier. As both parents were no longer able to care for themselves they reluctantly agreed to my hiring daytime help to take care of cooking, cleaning, and shopping. And, as the situation worsened I added coverage so that someone was there 24/7.

In the past 6 months, I have moved my parents from their apartment in Maryland to a new apartment in my building in NJ. I am exhausted from the volume of work and details associated with this change in circumstance and from worry. What is driving me today is that I have recently found out that the current aide, who is smart, is a great cook, and appears attentive whenever I am there, is using their credit card and leaving them alone at night while she travels to another city to see friends. When I confronted her she lied, even when proof was presented to her. As I speak, my distress, and longing to keep my parents safe and well-cared for, is evident. Jeff listens, nodding and interspersing more Uh-huhs.

At times the look on his face softens in response to my struggles. I continue to talk about being dependent on the aides and how I can't trust them. As I continue to tell the story I speak of getting really anxious, and my voice tightens.

Jeff, in a calm anchoring state, keeps his eyes fixed on my face.

S: It reminds me of an A. A. Milne poem, when she was good she was very very good and when she was bad she was terrible.	As I speak I gesture, Jeff nods emphatically as if to punctuate my statements.
Um...so some of it, as I'm talking to you...is letting go of control because I feel like I should be able...I feel like I should be able to hire people who are going to keep my parents safe and who are going to be truthful to me and maybe that's not possible... everybody I talk to says aides lie.	
I don't know.	I toss my hands up in the air while resting my arms on the arms of the chair.
Jeff: Mm-hmm...right...so right now, you're stuck...mm-hmm...	In a loving and kind voice, which is in stark contrast to my anxious tone.
S: Yeah, I'm doing that...I noticed that, because I'm so focused here	My anxious tone diminishes slightly at his mirroring
...that I don't feel as stuck	My tone of voice belies this, I am still stuck
and also I'm not in daily interaction with my parents...and I'm not...so I'm not as worried about them. Um...and I guess for me, being truthful is really important.	Hands moves back and forth, palms face in then press down, palms down

Jeff: Okay, well wait...let's explore it in a more unadulterated form.	Calm, in charge voice – Jeff has heard enough
	Jeff begins by holding both hands in front of him, palms up, moving them as if he is gently juggling something, perfect seeding for what is to follow.
So one hand...is keep the aides	Jeff raises right hand to near shoulder height, palm up, and bounces it a bit while the left is held still and somewhat lower. I mirror this movement although my hand is still.
and one hand is find different aides...is that reasonable?	Jeff raises and bounces left hand palm up while the right hand is lowered and still. I mirror this movement as well, keeping both hands raised and still with palms up in a clear demonstration that both have equal weight.
How would you divide the territory?	Jeff flaps his hands as he checks in with me to make explicit what I am already implicitly indicating with the lack of movement of my hands.
	Jeff returns both hands to his lap.

S: Yeah.	I respond continuing to have both hands extend, palms face up.
Jeff: Okay...so which hand will be which?	Jeff waves his left hand to focus my attention and punctuate the point, and then returns it to his lap.
S: This is keep, this is let go.	I bounce my right hand. I bounce my left hand.
Jeff: Okay...which one do you want to start with?	Gestures with left hand, then returns it to his lap.
S: Keep.	Brief pause, rolls both hands/wrists, and then gestures with right hand, as left fingers touch left shoulder.
Jeff: Okay...so start with keep and in an absolutely unadulterated form stay with keep as if you are an attorney for keeping the aides and you are presenting the argument in absolutely incontrovertible terms where no one could possibly object to any aspect of the argument.	Jeff's left hand gestures toward me, right is in his lap... left hand waves in a circular fashion, thumb up and back of hand facing me, the movement changes as if to emphasize his words. His voice becomes staccato, head nodding emphatically, and hand movement shifts to horizontal slicing. He knows that I can be slippery and go off in other directions.

S: So, you want me to do this aloud?	I remember bracing myself and wondering how I can speak clearly about only one view. And, since I often prefer to go inside rather than verbalize I ask if I "have" to speak out loud.
Jeff: Yeah.	His head nodding emphatically, hands returned to lap.
S: Okay...so um...	Continuing to face Jeff, my voice somewhat flat, implying that I really don't want to do this.
Jeff: And it might even be interesting if you uh, talked to your hand, unhuh...yeah...	Infusing voice with curiosity and invitation, raises his right hand and looks toward it for a moment before returning it to his lap. This lightens things up a bit, externalizes the process and gives me something concrete to interact with.
S: Or my hand talk to me.	Speaking in a somewhat playful tone I bring my hand closer to my face and wiggle my fingers, then make a fist.
Jeff: Unhun… Ok... either way.	Nodding, both hands in lap.

S: Um...so...they're familiar with K...she keeps the house beautifully...she cooks beautifully...she, for the most part, stays on top of the medicine...	Holding my right hand up and talking toward it, I speak about the reasons why I should keep the aide. Jeff watches me with a serious look on his face, nodding occasionally.
She has limited ability to leave, use my parent's money anymore cause she knows I'm watching the card and I'm going to be taking the card when they come back so that she won't be able to do the charges anymore.	I keep my hand up but turn to look at Jeff who nods more vigorously
Jeff: Ok...so you're talking to your hand, you're explaining the argument for keeping, what's her name?	In a firm voice, accompanied by downward slicing motions of his hand. I am sure Jeff knew her name and was simply making me say it to vivify her.
S: K.	My hand stays raised, elbow resting on the arm of the chair

Jeff:	Raising his right hand, in a mirror image of mine, Jeff softens his voice, looks at both me and his hand and speaks.
K...ok...so um...now um...allow your hand for a moment to resonate...move with the energy of that argument	
	As he says this he rotates his right hand, almost in a come hither way and then drops it in is lap, having it rest over his left hand.
...so as if your hand has been absorbing that argument...	
	Changing the cadence of his voice so that it is more lyrical Jeff begins an induction which is accompanied by the movement of his hands first moving just his right hand.
your hand has been absorbing that energy...	
your hand has been absorbing that logic...and allow your hand to move somehow in a way that expresses its resonance and	He adds movement of his left hand so that they are both moving in sync.
the strength of the resonance with that argument...	
	Jeff lowers his right hand and just moves his left in a circular fashion.
	Then raising of both hands to waist height and turning them from palm down to palm up, repeating this a few times.
	Jeff reverts to only gesturing with right hand.

S: And it feels more like sort of a sadness and acquiescence... than...	As I speak I lower my right hand to my left knee which is crossed over my right leg. My left hand remains on my left shoulder. Jeff's hands are in his lap. My voice drops and is laden with sadness... My hand moves to and rests on my thigh.
Jeff: Fine...ok so hold onto that sadness, hold onto that acquiescence...feel that...	Jeff shakes his head and assumes a soft gentle voice. He takes his right hand and slaps it down on his right leg which is crossed over his left leg in a mirror image of mine.
S: Yeah...there's...	Deep in process, I pause with head slightly down then nod.
Jeff: ...wait...let's try the other side...	Jeff raising his left hand and looking at me he says in a declarative yet warm voice, knowing that both sides of this conundrum need to be heard and vivified.
S: Ok.	Keeping right hand resting on my left knee I take my left hand off my shoulder and hold it out, with my elbow supported by the arm of the chair. I continue to look at Jeff.
Jeff: And in an unadulterated way, as if you were the attorney for the prosecution in this case...	Gesturing with his left hand, in a circular motion, head slightly tilted to his right, his voice a bit more staccato and commanding.

S: No wait, Before I jump there...cause it feels like there's a resignation to not being able to trust...here...so I just want to keep with that so...	Patting my left knee with my right hand. My voice a bit anxious. As my voice trails off I turn my head to look at my left hand and Jeff reaches out his right hand toward my raised hand, eyes on my hand, joining me in my gaze.
Jeff: Well I think that goes more on this side...I'm resigned to the fact that she is not going to be trusted...	As he begins to speak, Jeff gestures again to my left hand then drops his right hand into his lap. Using both words and gestures Jeff keeps the two polarities separate and distinct.
S: ...So...I'm...	Continuing to look at my left hand.
Jeff: Unadulterated...	In a clear commanding voice; not letting me off the hook.

S: I know, I know...it's hard to get there...ok...um... ...you're never gonna be able to trust K...look at the family she comes from ...look at the fact that she's done all these things and lies to your face...um...you may as well get rid of her...and then... but staying here is really hard because I went through seven aides before I got K. It's hard to find anyone to trust and I really want to trust.	In a somewhat bemused tone with a hint of underlying amusement I say... With something less than real conviction in my voice and moving my raised left hand back and forth, closer then further from my face. I emphasize my point by pointing to my left palm with a finger of my right hand. As I say this I turn to look at my raised right hand that now is elevated higher than my left hand. Both elbows rest on the arms of the chair. Then I turn to face Jeff and in an incredulous voice I say:
Jeff: Ok...so you'll go back there...	Jeff nods, understanding what is at the heart of my dilemma, and then extends his left hand toward my raised right one and says in a kind voice:

S: Yeah...so you know, you went through seven aides...do you... it was exhausting...it was frightening to have people in there that you didn't trust to have your parents safe with...at least K keeps your parents safe most of the time.	In a resigned and tired voice I look off into space, neither looking at Jeff or my raised right hand which I move back and forth as I speak, palm turned toward my face.
...but it's interesting, it's not so much the decision about this, cause I trust that I'm going to come to some decision...	I talk some more. Jeff nods, I pause, then begin to move both hands back and forth in an alternating fashion away from and closer to me. Jeff nods signaling that he is with me.
Jeff: Ok...so what's it about?	
S:	I bring both hands closer and close fingers.
... It's the internal sensation...	I put my hands in front of my heart.
Jeff: What is the internal sensation?	Jeff's hands at rest.
S: Grggghhh...and just that...	I shake my hands.
Jeff: You are in betwixt...	Jeff raises his hands over his head and rapidly looks back and forth between them to dramatize his statement and utilize my gestures.

S: Well not between that...no, about lying...and about lying makes me feel like I'm on quicksand...and, I get some kind of confusion that makes me think there's something that's been a fellow traveler for a long time... that I would like to escort off the train...um, or at least train into some other behavior...	I throw my hands up momentarily and then drape them over the arms of the chair. I gesture with left hand to emphasize.
Jeff: Ok...well, help me to understand...what is wrong with hyper-reacting to lies?	Jeff isn't buying my facile use of words, and in a serious tone slowly says... He raises both hands and moves them back and forth in front of him before having them come to rest in his lap.
S: Well, it cuts out the possibility of a fair number of relationships cause most people tell some form of lie.	I pause then say:

Jeff: Yes...well there are degrees of lies...	Nods his head in agreement.
there are felony lies	
...there are misdemeanor lies	Uses his hands moving out and waist high as if conducting or marking the territory, he does this each time he states each type of lie and then returns his hands to his lap.
...there are sweet lies...convenient lies...and if...if a wife says to a man do I look good today?	
So there's some degree of lies that you hyper-reacted to... what's the problem?	My hands gesture as his did a few times and I nod each time he speaks of a category until he gets to the last type of lie. I shake my head as he gets to this point and he picks up on this. He pauses for a moment as I gesture a few times circling with my hands.
	I bob my head and begin to wag my pointer finger on my right hand.
S: See I would probably not want to be lied to if I asked someone if this looks good on me.	Looking up I say, slowly as if formulating a thought:

Jeff: Ok. So there is a demand, a request, an expectation or all of the above for integrity...absolute integrity...ok, now are you willing to give that kind of integrity?	Keeping his eyes on my face and his hands in his lap says in a solemn voice:
S: I make every effort to do that.	I nod.
Jeff: Uh-huh...so this is a really important value to you.	I nod again.
S: Mmm-hmm...	My posture becomes more rigid and my breathing is shallow. My eyes are riveted on Jeff.
Jeff: And a central value.	S: Mmm-hmm...
Jeff: How does it feel when I reflect that back?	Jeff moves his hands back and forth, fingers pointing up, as if he is mirroring the connective dance that we are sharing. His words are spoken in a gentle voice.
S: I feel sort of a straightening inside ...and a sadness that I, with the exception of a few friends, haven't found it anywhere.	My voice drops and my breathing is fuller. My left hand moves up and down the center of my body from the base of my neck to my belly and back.
Jeff: ...who values integrity and would say D, all of the above.	Sewing a bit of confusion yet generating resonance.
S: Yeah.	Nodding...

Jeff: This is an important sorting device...so you could be this open	Hands apart,
or this open	hands open wider,
or this open, depending on whether you found somebody who was able to meet your values as far as integrity was concerned.	arms spread wide apart, inviting me to modulate my expectation and experience rather than living from a one size fits all place.
S: Yes...I think the problem is that I'm this open and then I get confused ...probably a child state... when I realize that people are disingenuous...	As I am listening I sit in an open position with my arms resting on the arms of the chair. I begin with gesturing with my left hand, pointer finger extended, then spread my arms wide, then I rest my elbows on armchair. Hands point up and then the left gestures to indicate about 2 feet off the floor, then both hands back up. Arms rest on the chair.
Jeff: Uh-huh...so there is an expectation and some naive belief that people are going to hold integrity with the same degree of reverence that you hold it.	Gestures with left hand, gestures with both hands then bounces them, almost as if he is holding integrity as he speaks.

S: Mmm-hmm...yeah...	Continuing to gesture with both his hands, maintaining a relaxed posture.
Jeff: And then when people don't seem to have that value, you get pixelated...yeah.	
S: Yeah.	Eyes fixed on Jeff.
Jeff: Ok so now I'm just reflecting back to you what it is that you're saying to me and, as you process that...whereas...you have been like this	Using both hands, palms up to gesture. Arms spread wide apart.
...and then if somebody engages in any degree of deception, suddenly you're like this	Jeff rocks his upper body side to side, arms remain up for about 4 seconds then stops and returns his hands to his lap and watches me patiently, mirroring my still position.
S: Yeah and I also think that I tend to do that or be reactive and then go back into expecting that they're going to be honest and truthful.	My hands dance as I talk, a recapitulation of Jeff's movements.

Jeff: And if you were seeing your expression at that moment, it lit up...your eyes lit up and you smiled as you talked about going back into an expectation perhaps classified as a naive expectation...that everybody will hold sacrosanct your value about honesty.	His demeanor softens as mine does. Gestures with his hands, moves his torso back and forth. Jeff smiles. He tilts his head and raises his eyebrows. He continues to smile in a loving manner as he talks and gestures. I intersperse his comments with "Yeah."
Jeff (cont'd): As if everybody would hold sacrosanct your value about spirituality or travel or money or...	There is a mischievous smile in his eyes and voice as he continues. He is amplifying the absurdity of this and I haven't caught up with him yet, remaining in the concrete and specific.
S: As you were talking, I flashed on...losing it after 911 when somebody stole my parking space and so my sense of judgment— I mean not judgment, that's interesting...justice...	My voice begins to tremble. Two fingers of my right hand press against my temple and my left hand gestures in a circular movement.
Jeff: Yeah...thank you Freud.	Loving smile on his face and lilt in his voice as we share a bit of laughter.

S: Yes...pretty funny...it feels almost as if there's a part of me that is calcified...probably not the right word...but stuck back in a really young age that thinks that the world should be, and of course it's not...	My hands gesture, making a box shape, eyes are down cast. Looking back up at Jeff who has had his eyes on me the entire time.
Jeff: Yes...it's been also, looking at the virtue of that particular orientation...it's been a great sorting device...and it gives you some idea of whether you want to be some degree.	Jeff's hands raise as he talks and spread wider and wider apart to dramatize my ability to choose just how open I choose to be.
S: It would if I used it as such...	

Jeff: Oh, I have no doubt that you've been using it as such. ...now, we know, like I had Paul Ekman ...great expert on facial emotion and lie detection ...and he came to one of the Erikson conferences and he showed us pictures... micro-expressions of people who are telling the truth and people who are lying, and we wanted to see how did the thousand therapists in that ballroom do...	Jeff's tone is challenging, bringing both his clarity and his "BS" meter to bear. He shakes his head. I respond by moving my head back and forth on an angle as if saying maybe as Jeff gestures with his right hand. There is a pause and Jeff continues gesturing with both hands. I nod, remembering Ekman; Jeff smiles as he speaks. Jeff's hands raise as he evokes the image of the slides and video that Ekman presented and points to different places in the air as if drawing my attention to the differing images. He waves both hands over his head then gestures with his left hand.
S: And I didn't do great on the post-test either...	I light up as he speaks, and gesture with my thumbs down.
Jeff: Because, well this is an earlier conference...in San Francisco I was thinking, 1988...	Jeff readjusts his body, sitting more upright in chair and leans forward, gesturing with right hand.
S: Oh ok.	My arms rest on the chair, hands pointing down; relaxed and rapt.

Jeff: Something like that...so... he was absolutely clear that therapists absolutely suck at lie detection... that we naively expect that our clients are always going to be telling us the truth ...so it may be something in there from your childhood, and there can be something in there that's been certainly reinforced by the exigencies of our profession...	His shoulders scrunch with arms gesturing in an animated fashion, palms up. There is a lilt to his voice as if he is sharing a secret that tickles him. I nod. He raise both hands and moves them back and forth in small movements as if juggling.
S: Mmm-hmm...	I purse my lips.
Jeff: So what you don't want to do is you don't want to be so pixelated...	Raising both hands and gesturing slightly.
S: Exactly.	
Jeff: By people who are engaged in any degree of deception.	He continues to make small gestures with both hands, then his hands come to rest.
S: Right...and I mean if a client lies to me, you know... it's their nickel basically but if a friend... yeah...I don't want to be so pixelated by all the other lies that will come across my path...	I toss up hands.
Jeff: Uh-huh...so there's some categories...	He nods and raises his hands and moves them back and forth—palms facing each other as if marking the space.
S: Yeah.	

Jeff: About what kind of lies are pixelating...	Raises hands and makes a similar motion palms facing each other, marking the territory then hands go back to his lap.
S: Well I think that every category pixelates but to a lesser degree...	I pause, thinking.
Jeff: Mmm-hmm...	
S: If someone said, oh...I can't do this because of blah, blah, blah and it turns out that blah, blah, blah wasn't true...um...you know that might be one level of pixelation, and then we go up to aides charging a couple of hundred dollars for cab rides...$600 I think it was total...um...yeah...	I use my hands, palms down to make the levels, picking up on Jeff's use of his hands.
Jeff: For $600, you could get a ride from here to Peoria.	Said in a wry tone of voice, holding back a smile. I speak a bit more about details, Jeff waits kindly.
Jeff: So that to you is a felony lie...	I absorb this and pause, struggling to nail it all down in my mind. I speak a bit and Jeff solemnly replies.
Jeff: Mmm-hmmm...serious misdemeanors...	
S: Yeah...	Still caught in the seriousness of it all.

Jeff: Mm-hmm...and so, help me to understand... does it make sense that you should have some sorting system that is reactive when you sense deception...beep, beep...	He begins again to utilize his hands to act out an accompaniment to his words. Hands stop moving.
S: Yeah...	I nod.
Jeff: Mm-hmm...but what you want to have is beep beep beep...rather than being some doe-like, frozen in time...ok...	Hand again illustrating a sorting system; I nod.
S: I think I get anxious but I deal with it...and I want to not get anxious about it... I want to... ok...I want to de-personalize it.	Talking over Jeff. Jeff hits the right side of his head..
Jeff: Ok...de-personalize it.	Crosses legs at knee, mirroring me. Hands clasped in his lap. Mine on arms of chair.
S: Yeah...cause I take it personally.	
Jeff: Uh-huh.	Nodding, encouraging me...
S: And um...	
Jeff: Taking it personally is what...help me to understand that...	Gesturing with hands that he keeps clasped.
S: I feel like it's a judgment of my worth and you know our relationship and um...	
Jeff: I'm going to do an action.	Jeff circles his hands and seeds this next step.

S: Ok.	
Jeff: ...This is my best rendition of St. Vitus's dance.	Jerks his arms and body up several times, as if he is having a fit of some kind.
S: St. Vitus's dance?	
Jeff: Yeah...it's a gross neurologic that cause tics...tic disorder... neural discharges... and the person has tics... So if somebody has St. Vitus's dance ...and they have neurological discharges...they might have tics...where's the worst place to stand?	He repeats gesture of thrusting hands above head and jerking his body a number of times. He repeats the tic.
S: Close to them, I would think.	
Jeff: Mmm-hmm.	Nodding...
S: Very elegant...	I look up, then at Jeff. Laughter, nodding and sharing the chuckle with Jeff. I then get quiet, letting the work settle in me.
Jeff: Strange how an image can become indelible.	
S: Yeah...well, how indirection can be so powerful.	
Jeff: Mmm-hmm...orienting towards.	
S: Yeah...so I feel sad but I feel almost...not almost...a physical release.	My hands move up and down the front of my body.

Jeff: Yes.	
S: And relief.	
Jeff: Ok...so hold onto that for a moment...feel it, enjoy it... and consider it as the um...way in which a reorganization happens.	My hands are raised and moving in a circular fashion. "Happens" is emphasized with a twirl of his right hand.
S: Mmm-hmm...	
Jeff: And that there's an organismic sense, "whooo...aha..." and organismic sense of reorganization. Like the sound of the wind.	His hands continue to dance.
S: And so my brain—and it's funny cause it feels like it's right over here—	I pause and speak slowly, I point to the left side of my head with my left hand.
Jeff: Uh-huh...	
S: Is saying the other piece of this, which—	My left hand undulates then returns to the chair arm.
Jeff: Piece is good...	A wonderful double entendre: "peace/piece."
S: —weaves in is that when the person in question comes back and acts as if nothing's wrong and is sweet and lovely...um... unlike the cobra...that they have been... and so I get to overlay the St. Vitus dance on their warm presentation because...	Index finger of one hand makes circling gesture. Doing the tic movement a few more times.

Jeff: Very intelligent...	Nodding emphatically.
S: ...	Deep breath out.
Jeff: ...that is a deception about the deception.	Head tilted to the right and gesturing with his right hand.
S: Yeah.	
Jeff: It's stipple.	Does the St Vitus's dance a few more times.
S: Yup...and so there's this young part of me that's saying yes but, yes but... ...that wants to believe the deception and so that part gets to step behind me, so to speak... instead of leading the show.	Pointer finger on right hand raised and stabbing the air.
Jeff: And what is she about? And why would she want to believe the deception? She would want to believe that the world is Disneyland and that everybody gets an e-ticket...that would be really sweet and really age appropriate... for a little girl.	Gesturing with both hands as if unpacking a box with both hands working simultaneously. Gestures with left hand.
S: Yeah...for a little girl.	
Jeff: Mm-hmm...	
S: So...what I'm doing is talking to her about the fact that um... you don't need pretend friends anymore...	I'm quiet for a bit, then speak:
Jeff: Brilliant...	He says gently.
S: Um...and I think she did because that was her only option when she was little...	Nodding.

Jeff: Pretend friends can be trustworthy, loyal, helpful, courteous, kind, obedient, thrifty, friendly, brave, clean, and reverent...	Nodding. Moves his right hand – and I mirror this.
S: Or not...	We both nod.
Jeff: ...that was the Boy Scout oath by the way.	Raising his right hand and points up with two fingers.
S: I got that...and I flipped to one of my major tormentors' mother in our Girl Scout troop and I quit because it was so obnoxious but anyway...	With both hands flopping.
Jeff: Let go.	Jeff doesn't get sucked in by this trip into specificity. Waving his left hand.
...So how do you see her and how do you talk to her and,	Using both hands he moves them back and forth at midline, palms facing in.
how do you help her to recognize	Turns hands so that palms are facing up as he moves hands in a circular fashion.
that what was once age appropriate is now no longer useful or desirable?	

S: Um...it's gonna be a work in progress because right now, she doesn't want to hear it... um...when I was driving in with Hank I was talking a little bit about what I was going to work on and that it felt like it was a...I'm going to get the word wrong again...	Hands dance, simulate weaving, drawing a box and then coming to rest.
	Touch my left temple with my left index finger.
...and I don't know why...confabulation	Touch my left temple with my left index finger.
...not confabulation...it's conflation...	Hand at desk height level.
	Hand slightly higher.
...when things are kind of woven together so it's... or you're missing the distinct boundaries so it feels like it's a really young part about this big	Jeff nods but there is a sense that he's getting ready to stop this train.
...but then the part this big	I pause then continue in a trembling voice.
...that it grows out of an amalgam of thoughts and disappointments and	Jeff raises his eyebrows at this, an old and oft worked theme for me.
...um...but I also feel really tender toward all of that...in me... and the voice I hear right now is...you don't have to try so hard...	

Jeff: So experience the resonance of that voice...you DON'T have to try so hard... YOU don't have to try so hard... you don't have to TRY so hard...you don't have to try SO hard...you don't have to try HARD...and then there may be the realization that that's a sentence stem: you don't have to try so hard to...	Voice softening and gentle. Gesturing with both hands, moving them as he comes to the emphasized word and then resting them again.
S: It feels like it's almost everything...to keep my parents safe... to get things right. . . ...I mean I could have...262 pages that Jim did on that...	Long pause, then I speaks softly. I use my hands to emphasize each statement as Jeff has done in unconscious resonance.
Jeff: Uh-huh...yes...ok well stay with that for a moment and feel the intensity of that software... and the software program was you HAVE to try so hard...	Opening and closing his hands as they rest on his lap. Notice his choice of words. He could have said program but he chose to use the word software—something that is malleable and mutable and, well, soft.
S: It's really interesting because I feel such relief and my body feels so relaxed and open right now...	
Jeff: Mmm-hmm...	Nods.

S: ...that I'm more bemused by that software and I can see where it came from...	
Jeff: Mmm-hmm...	Nods.
S: And I can...elect to ...modify that program...	Wiggling my fingers.
Jeff: Do you think that there was something about that program that was...	Nods. Repeats St Vitus's Dance several times.
S: Oh yeah...yeah...	
Jeff: And that it can be interesting to recognize that trying too hard to succeed is a form of self-deception...	Hands moving back and forth again, first one then the other. In a gentle voice:
S: That will have to sit for a while cause my brain is not parsing that out in any way that would make sense...	I pause, absorbing this.
Jeff: Sit with it for as long as you want... think about whether or not what I'm saying has validity...	Nods emphatically, voice more firm. Hands moving back and forth.
S: The fact that I'm in a brain fog tells me that it has a great deal of validity...	Pausing and looking off to the right. Jeff nods repeatedly.

Jeff: That there are some ways that we deceive ourselves	Moves both hands one at a time in small circles.
...predicting an unpredictable future or trying to...working or...	Gestures with both hands together to emphasize.
let me see...having a program of perfection	
...or any one of a number of different programs...that if we don't take time in this context	Hands raised and gesturing in a way that links the two of us.
...to examine those self-deceptions, that we are all privy to	Continues to use hands that are raised just above his lap as the base note to his words
...I can say it in a gentler way, that one of the papers in Confluence is about heuristics and that we pick up heuristics, simplifying assumptions about therapy, about life...and that some of those simplifying assumptions become programs in our mind and if we don't take time to examine them, we keep on doing the same things...so part of the purpose of that paper was that for one month, I wrote out all of the heuristics that I was using for induction, for deepening, for trance work	Left hand makes rolling gesture forward. Arms spread wide. Using right hand to mark out items on his leg starting closest to his body and moving out.
...or family therapy and I just had categories of looking at the heuristics that I was using and I don't know how	

Jeff (cont'd): many heuristics I wrote out...certainly more than a hundred...and then dusted them off and realized that some of them were self-deceptions... and that they really didn't have any validity...and then my recommendation to myself was to examine on a more frequent basics,

what are some of the heuristics that I'm using to see if there was validity to them or if they were just superstitions and self-deceptions...so this is... What you opened up is a side door to something else that you may want to consider...which is trying too hard to succeed to succeed. And then...when you knock on the door of deception as it's happened to you, suddenly you come out that side door into this other room which is trying too hard to succeed to succeed...and I'm considering a self deception...

S: Mmm-hmm...so I get lost in the words because I get...trying so hard to succeed... ...ok...touché...so then that just brings me to a place of stillness.	Laughing, and the room joins us in the laughter. I kick my feet a few times as I laugh. Jim's baritone laughter raises above the background and Jeff leans forward to meet me as we continue to laugh.
Jeff: Yeah, and pensiveness and thoughtfulness and that you could take your time with this one and feel your way through it... and see where it takes you...and suddenly there was a little bit of pixelating moment when you found yourself trying too hard to succeed to succeed...you might pay attention to it...	Gestures with both hands. I'm not there, as my mind is still, too. He is back on target and gestures with both hands.
S: It's funny cause trying too hard to succeed to succeed feels like it could be a koan...um...and when I try to wrap my mind around it...	Long pause, arms resting on the chair. Jeff sits more upright, leans forward slightly.
Jeff: As a self-deception?	Jim chuckles in the background.
S:... As even a phrase... I just get confused, which is ok...	I say emphatically, tossing up my hands. Jeff chuckles, as do I, as I lean forward.

Jeff: Uh-huh...see the thing that Dr. Erickson wrote in the first book that I gave him 40 years ago, was December, 1973...and I gave him...*Advanced Techniques of Hypnosis in Psychotherapy* in which he wrote, "Into each life some confusion should come... also some enlightenment"...as if the former was the precursor of the latter...	Gesturing with right hand held high and smiling. As he speaks he uses his left hand to emphasize certain words. I nod and smile. I continue to smile and nod then dip my head in acquiescence. Jeff returns his raised right hand to his lap.
S: Ok...	Nodding.
Jeff: And sometimes by just allowing things to cook a little and simmer and I have every good faith to entrust that you will cook things and think about things and come to some good place with it.	Smiling with his eyes and his voice he uses his hands to dance above his lap. I begin to nod.
S: Yeah.	
Jeff: And that what you're doing is...what I said...it's like you open one door and suddenly a side door appears, or another metaphor is, if you take off a layer of the onion, you may find something else...that appears underneath it...	Hands circumscribing his words, they then come to rest in his lap as he finishes the sentence.
S: Yeah...this feels really, really pivotal for me...um...yeah.	Jeff nods.
Jeff: And that's good.	

S: Yeah.	Nodding.
...and I do love the sense of hubris that sort of bubbles up when I think about expecting people to follow my rules...	One hand lifts towards my face.
Jeff: Uh-huh...	
S: Which doesn't mean that I can't expect and require that people who work from me not steal from me...	
Jeff: Right...absolutely...two different things.	
S: Yeah. But that's also from a different place.	
Jeff: And hubris seems like a little harsh...but it's the kind of naiveté of a little girl expecting things to be Disneyland...and um...	Puts a finger from his right hand to his lips. Motioning that hand in circles.
S: You mean they can't be?	My head juts forward, laughing, playfully, others laugh and Jeff smiles and pushes his chair back a bit.
Jeff: Only in Athens.	He chuckles as he makes a rolling movement with two fingers on his raised right hand.
S: Or Singapore.	He nods his agreement. I smirk. Jeff puts his head down and appears to be thinking.

Jeff: So...just as an editorial side bar, like as a therapist,	Continuing, Jeff waves his right hand near his head then moves his right hand to his chin.
and I think I've used this example before...sometimes you say something to somebody and you're trying to reach the baby... cause Rob and I were talking about parts...and in doing so, you offend the child...a less archaic part, and sometimes you say something to the child in a person and you offend the baby and that there's...you know when you were talking about	Gestures with right hand. Continuing to gesture with right hand.
...these little series of ego states that exist inside you from various ages, I thought that was a very apt and intelligent metaphor,	One hand gestures up steps. I nod, Jeff continues to hold the right hand raised, and left hand marking his words.

Jeff (cont'd): because there are those little fixations in time that have happened that leave us with patterns and little ruptures that we need to examine so... deception, that could be something that offends the baby	I nod.

Jeff gestures with left hand. |
| ...trying too hard to succeed to succeed could offend the child or be (ir)relevant* to those different stages | His right hand raised and gesturing.

*Not sure which word he used, both work. |
But—but I'm cutting it down to two but there's more...	
But—but I'm cutting it down to two but there's more...	Right hand moving back and forth.
S: It feels like the deception piece is...many different ages	Left hand gesturing, marking many different places; then I place tips of 1st two fingers of left hand on my chin and Jeff mirrors this with his right hand.
...that trying too hard to succeed to succeed probably	
...slightly different parts but still it's thrown out...but there's work that I can do with each of those ego states around it...	Jeff nodding.

Jeff: Yeah...and what I wouldn't want you to answer right away because whatever you said right away would only be part of the truth...the bigger truth—like there's a little t and a big T—	Continues with same gestures, speaking slowly and deliberately, modeling the behavior. Beautiful utilization and seeding.
...and so um...the um...more robust pattern...the more robust software program that would replace trying too hard to succeed to succeed	Enunciating each word. I look up and to the left as I listen.
...and that um...shouldn't be answered with your first answer... but something that could...cook inside you for a while and that you could feel and test and try on different resonant orientations...that would reflect more about who it is that you are now ...and who it is that you're growing into...	Emphasizing "YOU." Gestures with arms and hands wide and moving wider.
S: Then I might... ...cause I'm not going that way anymore ...but the openings...	Repeat Jeff's gestures. Right arm goes up and out. Arms again repeating Jeff's gesture. Deep exhalation.

Jeff: Mm-hmm...so that leaves it as a... um...as a seed, as an opening ...but not anything that I would need, or hope that you would need therapeutically, as clear definitive moment...	Hands gesturing again together in circular fashion. Both hands up, right circling.
S: No, It feels like something organic and what I want to move towards in this new program ...would be more flexibly responsive.	Arms resting on the chair; speaking slowly. My hands raise and gesture. Then I gesture with just my left hand. Jeff nods.
Jeff: Ok...well, try that on for a while and...see how that fits you.	Gestures with left hand.
S: And see how that works... ok. I can always tweak it... though I'm not very good at finding lines of code but...	Talking over Jeff. Nodding. Right hand dancing. I tap the chair with right hand—then rub the arms of the chair as I know that Jeff isn't going to follow me down that rabbit hole.

Jeff: Mm-hmm...does that feel good?	Head tilted to the side.
S: That feels excellent...	Tap arm of chair with right hand.
Jeff: It was really delightful to work with you this morning...I think it was important.	
S: Thank you...it was very important.	

As I review this transcript, I feel the warmth of the connection that Jeff invites with every cell of his being. I think of his laser focus and his genuine warmth, which shines through despite his inherent shyness and the massive demands that come from being "on" as a peripatetic mentor/teacher/therapist/friend. It is my hope that Jeff's creativity, his utilization of what I brought, on every level— words, gestures, breath, emotion, metaphor—has shone through as you read the transcript and that you were able to experience as I did the mastery and magic of Jeff's amalgam of experiential therapies. I want to leave you with an experience, nowhere near as elegant as Jeff's St Vitus's Dance, yet one that I hope will help you anchor and metabolize the essence of my experience of his work.

Take a moment and imagine a large box. You can feel the shape and heft of the box, you might be curious about what is inside as you become more aware of the way it has been designed. As you continue to explore the exterior of this box there is a dawning realization that this box, your box, holds your own, your personal, jigsaw puzzle. You can bounce the box in your hands, you can appreciate its weight, you can appreciate its structure, and you can really appreciate its design. You can be curious about the way that it has always been with you and anticipate what it will be like to look inside. As you take your next breath you can become aware of Jeff sitting across from you listening, deeply listening to you, deeply listening to you. And as he listens, he invites you to pick out the relevant pieces from your box reminding you that you can feel their heft, you can appreciate their texture, you can trace their contours, you can see their colors. As you take each piece out of the box Jeff explores it with you, using his body and all of his senses to help you use your body and all of your senses to really absorb the essence, the interrelatedness of the piece (peace). At times what you have drawn out fits nicely with the previous piece and there is a delicious clicking into place; the picture emerging as this occurs. Other times, the piece may be set aside at Jeff's direction, or placed on the board waiting for the right companion piece(s). At times, Jeff may look into the box and suggest that you withdraw a particular piece. And as if by magic, Jeff may reach into his box and bring out a story, an enactment, a sound that reaches into the depth of your being, setting off a delightful flurry of neuronal activity that feels a lot like your pieces shifting into just the right place.

Looking back on this session, I am reminded that the work that we do, because it is embodied experience, continues to move in us long after the session has ended, feeding us like the proverbial mountain spring that both nourishes and reconfigures the hillside as it travels down the slopes.

In closing I'd like to note that experiential therapies and master therapists abound; what makes Jeff unique, while difficult to summarize, is his amalgam of vital characteristics. He brings warmth and, where appropriate, playfulness, to each encounter, inviting everyone to be their best selves. He is exacting in his craft and is able to distill and teach the essential elements of his work and the work of the other masters of therapy in both a didactic and experiential manner that invites us to be expansive, experimental, rigorous, and playful. He continues to expand the bounds of therapy exploring parallel universes—film, music, art, social science—in his quest to embroider upon the whole cloth of healing arts. When working with others, he focuses on the positive and the emergent rather than on what pieces might be missed or are misaligned. In utilizing this approach he excites our imagination while minimizing the possibility of shame that can accompany our imperfect efforts—so many in our profession are recovering perfectionists.

CHAPTER THREE

Experience in a New State: Horsing Around Untethered With Some Friends in Central Park

Bette J. Freedson

At the Brief Therapy Conference in Orlando, Florida in 2010, one of the first people I ran into was my friend Rick Miller. I'd not seen Rick since closing my Boston practice where we'd run groups on intuition together. Rick had continued to practice in Boston while my husband Ray Amidon, a family therapist, and I were becoming established in Maine. As surprise and delight morphed into the business of catching up, I learned two big things about Rick: an Ericksonian approach had become Rick's clinical passion, and Dr. Jeffrey Zeig had become his mentor.

"I am presenting at this conference!" Rick told me.

"It's Jeff Zeig! He's done so much for me. I've been going to Master Classes in New York with him. I'm learning more about hypnosis and so much else. Jeff's amazing. You would love Master Class. It changes you! And you will love Jeff. You and Ray have to go—soon."

Ray and I had been to several of the Erickson Foundation's conferences. At the 2000 Evolution Conference, I'd been inspired to write the first notes for a book about single mothers. I'd attended workshops with Dr. Jeffrey Zeig, and found his teaching to be clear, accessible, and helpful. I'd watched him interact with both faculty and attendees with graciousness and genuine warmth. Dr. Zeig exuded intelligence and caring in large and small venues alike. I sensed there was something special about him; I respected Dr. Zeig—comfortably from afar; the idea of being in a master class with him was interesting—and intimidating.

Later that day after attending a workshop with Dr. Zeig, Ray and I decided to ask about the New York Master Class. To be truthful, I was nervous to speak to him—he was the renowned Dr. Jeffrey Zeig. He knew everyone who was anyone in the clinical world. Who was I to work with him? But Rick said... Of course we should come to New York. Get in touch with Helen Adrienne and sign up!

After Rick's endorsement and Jeff's warm and gracious welcome, my intention was sealed, and fortunately Ray's was too. I sensed that this was a pivotal decision. What I could not fully foresee was the way in which these master classes and having Jeff's wisdom and kindness in my life would change me.

Over the years Jeff has continued to guide me toward the curative force of this first Master Class session. He supports my accomplishments, encourages my potential, and always reminds me to believe that: "I Can!"

Jeff has become my master teacher, occasional therapist, respected and beloved mentor, supportive colleague, and a friend. However, let's return to May 2011, New York City, when the experience was new, and the infusion of creativity into my work, the delight of having new friends in my life, and the deepening of trust in my true self were gifts yet to be opened.

Discovering Resources in a New State

When Ray and I arrived at Helen Adrienne's office for our first Master Class, I was clueless as to what was going to happen. Perhaps I had not heard Rick tell me, or had blocked the fact that we each "performed" therapy in front of everyone and would be working on our own issues! Perhaps my unconscious saved me, for had I consciously known the protocol, I might have been too scared to say, "Yes!"

All I wanted was to survive the next four days, and maybe learn a little along the way. I could not have imagined that I would learn how to take meaningful steps into new states of creative potential, find the courage to honor my passion for life, and be proud to acknowledge my authentic Self.

My first venture into Master Class has now expanded into years, as well as numerous experiential and didactic classes and consultations with Jeff and my colleagues. Daring to write this chapter is another step!

I am proud to share my first experience in the NYC Master class, and my first encounter with the profound knowledge, deep humanity, and creative brilliance of Jeffrey Zeig.

The Hypnotic Power of Elicitation

During Thursday morning's flutter of putting Velcro name tags on a poster, I found myself putting my session with Jeff last on Sunday. After four days of nervously anticipating and enthusiastically participating, I was excited. What evolved during this last first session came as the amazing discovery of the resources in a new state of being myself.

B: I'm delighted to be sitting here with you and very privileged and when I signed up on Thursday I did not realize, I was scattered…where am I going to put my labels…and I would be the last one to sit here and since I did the work with Sue, early on, my mind has been a collage of images and memories, thoughts and feelings about being last, putting myself last.

Jeff in his Ericksonian wisdom does not zoom in on this metaphor directly. Immersed in his state of readiness to utilize what I share, Jeff observes, listens, and strategizes his landing. He is ready to elicit an alchemical transformation by spinning the phenomenology of my negative trance state into the curative healing of clinical gold.

B: And many pieces of that have come to me and I'm trying to find an umbrella, and the umbrella that I've come up with is that I would like to accomplish some progress in my feeling legitimate. In so many ways in my life I… held myself back, kept myself from, not allowed myself to feel like I belong, like I'm legitimate in my personal life, in my work life, and at the same time there's a voice in me that says, "That's ridiculous." Of course, some of that's my mother's voice because my mother would say, "Bette Jane, that's ridiculous."

J: Sometimes mothers should be listened to.

This short, targeted response is typical of Jeff: purposeful, thought out, and precisely on the donkey's "tale." His comment is an example of the therapist's state of being ready to utilize whatever the client brings into the session. Jeff utilizes my mother's words to help me begin to realize something about my negative trance, a mental schema of distorted beliefs and perceptions about my self-worth that form one taproot of my insecurities.

How simple, "Listen to your mother!" In a brief therapy context, this could have been the entire therapy! But a negative trance implies dissociation implies the cut-off from resources. This is in evidence as I oscillate between states, a dynamic that Jeff does not directly point out, but later reframes as normative in the context of a psychic wound.

B: Well, sometimes someone listens too much, although there were times she was probably right and I didn't listen.

Jeff was ready for the ambivalence and brings me to the positive side of the dissociation, a strategy intended to elicit resources.

J: So how are you legitimate? How did you belong in your family of origin?

Speaking with his special gaze, the one where his eyes smile and his mouth turns up just a bit, Jeff beams acceptance, implying that I am okay, that I am good enough to belong, to belong in Master Class, to belong to myself. He uses the word legitimate strategically to connote where he intends to take me.

In teaching, Jeff emphasizes the importance of being strategic, having a landing place and being ready to utilize the opportunities that will take the client to that destination.

Learning the skills to be in a state of readiness to utilize opportunities that take you to the landing is fascinating.

You must know where you want to go even when you do not know exactly how you'll get there. It's almost as if your own unconscious acts as an intuitive GPS, giving you the directions as you get to the next point. Jeff skillfully demonstrates the precision necessary to keep this delicate balance. He opens space for a response that might allow me to draw from reference experiences of being legitimate, beginning now to dissociate them from the morass of negativity into which I have been inadvertently induced.

This is also an example of Jeff using conceptual communication as well as a basic therapy tool of getting more information. Jeff is addressing not only my conscious mind, but also evoking a dissociative response from my unconscious mind, where he already knows a felt sense of legitimacy resides. All this is strategically intended to elicit the shift that will bring about a realization of achieved and innate legitimacy. This also strategically sets the tone for more therapy to come.

B: I was the first of two sisters...

J: Ah-huh. You had the territory. (*Speaking to my unconscious mind where I could know I came by this territory legitimately.*)

I am now feeling a bit less self-conscious and more comfortable sitting across from Jeff. The initial apprehension of performing, mixed with the intention to actually have a real therapy session with him, has morphed into a fuller engagement in the clinical actuality. Sensing Jeff's respect, genuine interest, and compassion conveyed with gesture and gaze, my angst is settling down. Looking at Jeff, I forget the group is looking at me. It is safe to share.

B: I had the territory, and my sister, who's also a therapist, still struggles with... And I carried some guilt about that even though, what could I do? But I had them for five years to myself, including grandparents, with whom we lived.

J: First born grandchild? (*Hardly illegitimate!*)

Jeff continues here with his strategy to bring forth acceptance of myself as legitimate.

B: Yes and then two cousins came right after me and they were not local, but that brings me to one piece of my story. Because... the mother of these two cousins was my Aunt Bea who was very dear to me, my mother's sister, and I always wished she was my mother. She had the gentleness that my mother lacked and I had two messages. I had, "Bette Jane, you're terrific," from my mother, and from my grandmother, but my father was fairly passive, but loving in his way... disturbed... not in a way that was overtly unkind or mean. He imploded; tried to kill himself when I was about 27... he was kind, but he was crazy in himself. My father's family had been very wealthy. In fact, the family story is that my father's father who was cold as dry ice...

The Magic of Metaphor

J: Burning cold.

At this point I am beginning, or more accurately continuing, to dissociate. On the conscious level I am quickly spilling out some details. As I recount disjointed parts of a painful story, my unconscious mind is working behind the scenes to fathom a concept, "legitimate."

Attuning to my eyes, my body posture, my breathing, and the staccato tempo of my speech, Jeff is observing me with that look that says, "I am holding you." Feeling held, I spill out my pain in a few furious details.

Exquisitely attuned to my shifts of attention that seem strobe-like ("spastic"), Jeff goes to the dissociated point with two precisely chosen words, "burning cold."

My unconscious may be beginning to realize that having a mentally ill father and a cold, uncaring grandfather may have contributed to a certain cold attitude I hold toward my self, a painful reality that, cut off from awareness, leaves me floundering at times in a negative Self-state.

Later, Jeff will come back to the pain by challenging me to own my own passion, and realize the humanness of having being negatively hypnotized within my family culture.

I have no conscious realization of Jeff's strategy, of course. And Jeff does not interpret overtly. As he tells us, never explain a magic trick. I am immersed now in the way Jeff's face radiates acceptance with a warmth that in itself can be healing.

I feel comfortable enough to explore the story of my father's side of the family. Unbeknownst to my conscious mind, my unconscious is exploring the truth of my worth.

Dissociation in the Service of Self-Compassion

B: Buuurrrrning cold. But not burning mean cold, [grandfather] just couldn't have cared about his grandchildren at all. (*I overtly play with the words and the disappointment and sadness of potentials unrealized, ideas and feelings elicited by Jeff's two juxtaposed concepts.*)

So story has it that he gave one of his poker players... $500 to buy a local movie theater, but didn't invest in it. And that man's name was Louie B. Mayer. So that's sort of the story. You know, [we] never had it, grandfather made it and lost it. Then it was all gone (*the money/the prominence*). So the story I was told in my life was we had it, but we don't have it anymore.

So, I get it now: it's scary to have it because you will lose it, and while my conscious knows my father was mentally ill, my unconscious mind gets the metaphor: my grandfather lost it all and my father lost it in more ways than one. Could this add up to, "You are a loser?"

And we... existed and did okay... but Auntie Bea... whatever the material piece was... had something that I wasn't getting in my family of origin. And I wasn't with her a lot, but when I was, I felt like I was really a person.

Eliciting the healing elixir of kindness

J: It was her kindness.

Jeff senses the importance of Auntie Bea. Her kindness. He already knows better than I do how unkindly I am likely to treat myself. Again, he is strategically precise, helping me stay within the dissociated realm of legitimacy. Now he adds a new ingredient to layer the experience, the concept of kindness, implying that with the comfort of Auntie Bea's kindness and her nonjudgmental posture, I might be able to absorb affirmation of my true self. But right now kindness toward myself is still spinning off in another orbit, currently dissociated from the universe of my total truth.

B: (*regarding Auntie Bea*) Her kindness, her smile, her gentleness, her respect… where my mother was directive and harsh, "Bette Jane, do this and do that," and my mother wasn't mean.

There would be many choice points in these statements. Jeff reminds his students that you cannot follow every point brought up in a session. He teaches us to build toward a chosen strategy, adding ingredients, attuning, layering, pacing, and increasing the impact to elicit the shift.

Another option might have been to ask for more elaboration about differences between mother and aunt, or the nature of harsh but not mean. One could question the way I might have absorbed a maternal directive that morphed into self-negation. None of this would be wrong. It is just that Jeff's chosen destination turned out to be right.

At this point in the session, kindness is also what I am experiencing from Jeff. This intentional emotional positioning is genuinely reflected in Jeff's voice, tone, and body language, as well as his questions and responses.

J: And what did Aunt Bea do?

With this question, I remember feeling warmth spread through me. By

*giving me space to talk more about Auntie Bea, Jeff offers me the oppor-
tunity to expand a positive emotion and the felt sense of acceptance (the
warmth I was feeling) from this positive reference experience.*

*This would also be interestingly interpreted from an object relations
perspective. But Jeff was heading down a different clinical path, taking
me into a new state where I could find where I had parked my central
core of self-love.*

B: Well, Aunt Bea would sort of sing my name. She would say, "BEtte, BEtteee..." and it just made me feel so good. And then there
was a time—and I've never said this to anybody except Ray—
when I was in the third grade and I was sick and I had diarrhea
and my teacher wouldn't let me go to the bathroom and I had
to go and I did and I was so mortified. And when I went home,
I was so grateful it wasn't my mother. She (Auntie Bea) cleaned
me up and loved me and took every bit of shame away. And that
was one of many times she gave me so much.

*I felt pretty exposed after this revelation, but the reality was that I was
already absorbed in a new trance state, and part of me was not worried about my disclosure. Now, more unconsciously in touch with what
was currently important, I switched topics and started talking about my
writing block.*

*In anticipating my work with Jeff, I'd hoped that my session might
unlock my inertia about finishing the book. Now absorbed in kindness
and acceptance from both Auntie Bea and Jeff, I begin to connect some
dots.*

B: I realize what's holding me back. Underneath the writing is, Do
I count enough? Am I smart enough? Does anybody want to
hear what I have to say? I have so much of it written. I realize
it's: Am I legitimate enough? Is my work enough? I mean this
room is filled with such brilliant, amazing people and you and
everyone—how can I even think that I could do what... I just
lose the words.

The only other piece is that... Ray says that I have so much bounty in my life that I don't know where to look first. In some ways, that's true. I feel so blessed. I want to be with my children, I want to be with my grandchildren, I want to be with my husband, and I love my work, I'm passionate about my work, I want to create.

J: Do you have friends?

Now with a simple question that a therapist might ask at any first interview, the placement of it here mildly destabilizes me as I am about to go back into the "Yes, but..."

Jeff is also utilizing his observations. For four days he has observed me enjoying reconnecting with Rick, and relishing my new associations in class, seeing me bond with Helen and others, beginning friendships that will last and deepen. Jeff utilizes his careful observations, and his intuition with a question designed to add another layer for the re-association of my often cut-off felt-sense of being enough.

B: I have a few. I don't have time for a lot, but the few I have I cherish. I feel like I have a whole new bunch of them today and this week. I feel so fortunate and so I'm pulled. Here, there, yon, there. And as a Gemini, and I don't know a lot about astrology, but I think it's in the Gemini major, from the little I know, that if I'm here, I'm like, "You should be over there." And it's not so much in my mother's voice...

Growth Factors—Destabilization and Dissociation

Here my dissociated self has one of its finest moments; and what Jeff says next utilizes dissociation in a way that is creatively and humorously destabilizing. He is going to bring me back to the point with intuitive precision.

J: Do you think you could go to Central Park tomorrow?

Central Park? We haven't been talking about that! Jeff often tells us to follow the "baby thoughts," a label for following intuitive ideas, something he attributes to Carl Whitaker. I am pretty sure this is what he was doing, and it catches me off guard as, of course, he intended.

With another layer of multilevel communication, Jeff suggests that I could go where I have "parked" my center of self. Obligingly destabilized, I respond from conscious mind.

B: Probably not because I promised my husband that we could go to Chinatown.

J: But you could have an image of Central Park. If you had an image of Central Park, what image would you have? Like, let's say you're standing across the street from one of the main entrances of Central Park, not on Central Park West or Central Park East. What's the street that runs north/south?

Here Jeff is using a confusion technique to get me to "the right place." The group enhances the effect, assisting Jeff in turning me around until he can get me to the designated Center place.

Group: 5th Avenue.

J: No, not 5th Avenue.

Group: Central Park West.

Someone: 59th Street.

J: 59th Street.

B: Well, I get the idea.

J: What is the idea?

B: I think the idea is to look, see what's there and where I am.

J: Well, you could have a muse in me, or you could have a muse in Bea, or you could have a muse in Milton Erickson, or your muse could just be a Central Park horse.

This is brilliant. An offer to be one's "muse" is powerful for a writer. He offers me the wisdom of his beloved teacher, Dr. Erickson, in a multitude of ways overtly and covertly. He offers me the choice to ride my own horse, to be my own person while continuing to have support. I am confused, but feeling solidly on my horse. Can Jeff know unconsciously how much I loved the "flying horses" at the amusement park as a child?

B: I did try riding horses when I was in my 20s.

J: So, what about a Central Park horse?

B: It would allow me to be part of the environment, as opposed to just flying through.

J: That would be something to muse on, instead of just being a Central Park horse.

More confusion, destabilization, and metaphor, as Jeff stays with the central Central theme, which seems to be also an interspersal technique used as a metaphor for following my own path. At this point my conscious mind is on one track, and my unconscious mind is doing quite a bit of work.

B: Well, if I were the horse as opposed to riding the horse, I don't know what a horse really thinks, but I assume that horses, like zebras, don't get ulcers. So I would probably be in the moment and I wouldn't be thinking about: What's on the other side and I better get there quickly. I probably wouldn't be thinking about was I enough? Do I look okay? Was I going to be laughed out of the room? Was I going to be thrown out of the group? I wouldn't be hearing my mother say....

I have just ridden into "Central Park." Recognizing this, Jeff offers an experiential moment for therapeutic effect.

J: There's an image that I've used myriad times so people here know it, you don't—which is this. (*Jeff taps his head.*)

Why am I doing this?

B: Not really sure. Probably you're autistic.

J: You don't know why I'm doing this?

B: No. You're knocking on your head.

J: Because it feels so good when I stop.

B: Oh, I understand that. I usually do it like this, banging my head on the wall. So, I'm not sure what that means.

J: So, you could entertain yourself with these curious thoughts about belonging and good enough, comparing yourself to any person hither and yon, right? And all that is... (*knocking on his head.*)

Jeff gives me a gift here. And I am dissociated enough to take it in—a metaphoric invitation to stop beating myself up. I get it but go back to the old beat. Jeff increases the tension to elicit a stronger shift.

B: Really good. It's like, "Oh, come on. Let's have a little bit of relief." Yeah, thank you. But I go back to it.

J: You could. Could you go back to it with the rhythm? Could you go back to it with a kind of harmony?

B: (*Laughing.*)

J: Like we've done this before but, you do this (*knocking on head*) right? So do it verbally – I'm not good enough, I don't belong, is there a place for me...da da da da da da da da...You can do that.

Jeff is increasing the tension here, utilizing another route to untether me from the negative trance that has a hold on me.

As Jeff has taught, down regulation can be overrated. Sometimes the shift will come from a state of increased arousal.

It is fascinating to me that Jeff seems to be using sounds, playfulness, and humor as a confusion technique to destabilize and increase dissociation as well as to inoculate me emotionally from the discomfort of his raising the tension.

B: I have to do the rhythm?

J: No, no. Just do it for the sake of doing it and do it in a kind of dizzying breathless way.

B: (*Singsongy.*) You don't belong, you're no good, nobody wants you, get with it, let's face the reality, you're stupid, or just not as smart as everybody else and what would they want with you.

J: Okay, uh-huh. Could you do that to a different tempo?

B: How about a little jazz, a little swing?

J: (*Making jazz sound.*) That would be like syncopation.

B: I'm not good. (*Sung in an arbitrary tempo.*)

J: Syncopation would be like you emphasize an unexpected beat. So rather than da...da da da da da, you would go dada daddaada, daddada.

B: You're no good. You're really stupid. I was thinking more of like a shuffle.

I'm well enough dissociated and in trance to be going right along with the "magic trick."

J: Try it.

Jeff has me in the palm of his hands, figuratively and literally. This must be how they do it in stage hypnosis. It feels like I am having a good time, horsing around with Dr. Zeig. Who'da guessed?!

B: You're no good, you're really stupid, and nobody wants to hear anything you have to say. Why would they listen to you when Jeff is in the room, or anybody else is in the room, or anybody in any place in the world? And then I would stop and I would say to myself, "You sound like a real idiot now." I can't get my bearings off it.

Indeed my bearings are quite destabilized, as Jeff brilliantly, playfully, and insightfully guides me to elicit a shift in awareness and perception. He skillfully uses my tendency to oscillate about my worth. I suppose he could have just said, "Tell me about your accomplishments," but that would be information for the conscious mind. Instead, Jeff hands the shift key to my unconscious mind.

B: It's not totally... I mean I'm proud of my accomplishments, I've come through a lot of adversity, I brought up two kids largely on my own. They're okay. They're minimally nuts, which is a pretty good thing, they're not involved in drugs, nobody killed anybody. I think, I feel like... when Harriet was working with you when I was crying, I felt like Harriet was like my soul sister and speaking my story in terms of allowing myself to do my heart's work, to sit and write the book. I'm writing articles on parenting and it's very satisfying. I love doing it. I'm doing workshops, I want to reach people and help women who are single parents.

I love doing that so much. I have all these metaphors... I wrote an essay called "Sparkle Plenty." I don't know if you remember who Sparkle Plenty was from Dick Tracy. Something that I sang with my friend next door. We sang: "Next to you, Gravel Gertie would have looked alright." So now am I Sparkle or am I Gravel Gertie? And so I don't know.

On My High Horse in Central Park—The Magic of Metaphor

J: Right.

"Right" is just a word on the page. But in person the delivery is the essence of Jeff creating impact. His expression, body language, and tone affects in me a sense of being ratified, of being heard and accepted. It's very significant in terms of allowing the shift to begin to be taken in and anchored.

B: And so maybe next to me Gravel Gertie would have sounded all right or sounded smart. So...

J: So there's been kind of a conspiracy here over these four days, and this conspiracy here is including you in it.

He's continuing to support absorption so that I can park the shift inside of my center.

B: Yeah, including telling me they think I'm okay, which is really hard to take in.

J: It's been a subterranean infusion.

Infusion to be confused with Confusion!

B: Um-hum. Conspiracy theory.

J: So that's like a reverse paranoia. Everybody's conspiring; they send us to include you in.

Brilliant use of the metaphor of paranoia: They are out to "get you—in!"

B: And Rick was involved. He was a perfect [inside] trader.

J: Absolutely. He's part of the conspiracy. So then, what that requires is for you to attune yourself to that entrainment.

(*The emotional/somatic attunement to the group's acceptance and respect.*)

Because here and it's here and it's been consistent over this period of time. So they're going to be our little chorus. And our chorus here has to do with good enough, good enough, good enough.

Now I have gone from feeling held, to feeling validated, back to feeling intimidated and scared; yet really wanting to be in the experience of this experience. With compassion and many levels of conceptual and poetic communication, like a kind grandfather or uncle, Jeff brings my new friends and me for a fun time in Central Park.

The Power of Entrainment—An Experiential Moment

B: Please don't make me say it. I think I'll die.

J: You have to.

B: Can I hold off for just a second?

J: Is it really important?

B: Yes, it's really important. I need to say this to you; you probably don't remember that we had a phone conversation. I was so embarrassed after that conversation. I said to Rick, "Oh my god, I told Jeff that I did psychic readings and I think he thinks I'm crazy. And I'm pretty sure that they're going to expect that I'm going to come on a broomstick." And Rick said, "Don't worry. You'll be okay." And I wasn't sure I could tell you this but in order to really, really get where I have to get I just really have to tell you that I was so worried that you thought I was some sort of complete nut. And then when my husband said, "Erickson didn't believe in psychics," I thought, "That's it. I'm out on a drum roll." I just had to say that.

I am getting untethered! Daring to reveal something important about myself, and daring to see if I will be accepted. Still scared.

J: Right. And what happened?

B: Nothing so far (*lots of laughter*).

J: All of that stress (*hitting his head*), all of that angst.

B: I thought I was going to die. I thought, "Oh my god. I said all the wrong things to him."

J: And it amounted to...

B: I worry. But I'm Jewish.

J: So, it's in your genes.

B: Have to. Have to worry. Please don't make me do it. Oh god.

J: Why?

B: Because I would be embarrassed.

J: As long as that embarrassment was an opening for you to begin to incorporate…

B: I'm not sure it is. Honestly, I don't know if I can stand it.

J: Well do it non-verbally. Okay. So everybody non-verbally is going to be doing this chorus. The chorus is being sent to radiate to you.

B: Can I ask a favor? Can I ask somebody to stand beside me and hold my hand?

Group: Absolutely.

B: Caroline. She's my Auntie Bea. (*Kisses Caroline's hand, crying.*)

J: And those could be good tears. And those could be the kind of tears that wash away the old patterns. Kind of tears that wash away old limitations. (*Points to Caroline.*) Could you take that chair? You can stop doing this mishegass. You can stop doing this mishegass. (*Utilization!*) And then suddenly, you are free and you're untethered from an orbit that has held you in stasis. (*More metaphor for the unconscious.*) So just by way of information, I'm clear that writing a book or doing a presentation has very little to do with being good enough. (*Information for my conscious mind and embedded suggestion for my unconscious mind.*)

B: I feel my best when I'm writing and presenting. I love it.

J: Yes, that's the important part. And so is your passion, your passion about presenting is what makes anything good enough. So, the intelligence, the analysis, the depth of thought, the cleverness of the metaphor is not what makes it good enough. What makes it good enough is the passion the person brings to the work. Having seen 30 years of evaluations of what people like in terms of presentations and directing two publishing companies, what makes it good enough is the passion that you bring.

And your message has passion. You radiate passion. So what you've been doing is you've been radiating passion and tethering yourself.

Thank you again, Jeff! You were tracking so perfectly and following the threads and utilizing what I gave you to land at this point where I could take in the therapy.

B: With the mishegass.

Now Jeff is going to make sure that the shifts get anchored so that I will have access to the new resources.

J: Right. And so then you've been at odds with yourself. And what we want to do in unison is to free you so that you are untethered and that you move forward with passion—and sometimes like a Central Park horse (*Jeff cups his hands over his eyes like blinders*). Somebody here may take a picture the next time they walk past so I'll email you that person so that you have a reference or strategy that works for getting some projects done.

B: You know it's interesting that you brought that image up because I just remembered that that was the image I used to get through the death of my ex-husband and my divorce, was the image of a horse with the blinders—just focus, put one foot in front of the other, and try not to look too peripherally. So, I thank you for reminding me about that.

J: Okay. That's good. So that's going to help. Untether yourself from that old mishegass, which just puts you at odds with yourself and puts you into a struggle with yourself, so that you're pitting your passion—what's excellent—against something that is archaic.

B: (*Turns to Caroline*) Will you stay there? I feel like I need to do this with someone beside me.

J: Okay. My way of doing it at the moment would be to conscript everyone here to amplify the message. And by virtue of amplifying the message, you can breathe it in.

B: I'll do my best to try.

J: Well, you've been a little spastic. Like I have a wound here or my appendix was taken out when I was 8 years old and if anybody tried to palpate that area other than myself I would tense up because I was wounded there. So I'm spastic in that area. Now, it doesn't change my life so I don't need to do anything about it. But if I did, I would have to do some work to open up that area, so that when somebody palpated that area I didn't tense up. I could just take it in for what it was designed to be. So, our over-arching message to you is about good enough. Or, could be, pursue your passion. Or it could just be Bette, how would you like us to phrase it.

B: I think pursue your passion.

J: Okay. So if it's a message that we would use the kind of Robb technique for, it would be: You can, Bette, pursue your passion. So we would put a little stress on the "you can," and then we would soften the voice, "Bette, pursue your passion." Could we have a rehearsal here? And, do we have any rhythm for that?

Helen: I have a drum.

J: We do? Is it filed under D?

Helen: Do we want to do this in two parts? One half does the...

J: You can.

Helen: And the other...

J: Pursue your passion. You can pursue your passion. So you're entitled? You are designed?

People: Destined. Destined. Destined.

Person: You may legitimately...

Person: Ah, I like that, that's good.

People: You may legitimately pursue your passion.

J: Okay, that's even better.

Man: And you can even do it illegitimately. Fuck it up.

J: Okay, so we have a drum beat? You can, Bette, legitimately pursue your passion.

Group: You can, Bette, legitimately pursue your passion.

J: In a softer voice. Soften the tone.

Group: (*Softer*) You can, Bette, legitimately pursue your passion. You can, Bette, legitimately pursue your passion. You can, Bette, legitimately pursue your passion.

J: Breathe it in. So now we're going to rephrase that and we're going to do that in tempo with Bette's breathing. So we're going to really attune ourselves to Bette as we're doing this. And then we're going to say our words... breathing is good.

B: I can't breathe.

J: So we're going to watch your breathing, and as you exhale, we're going to say: You can, Bette, legitimately pursue your passion. (*Group repeats and Jeff puts his hands on Betty's head.*) I'd like you to feel those things as if it were just something that was placed on your head. And it was there and it was guiding you and it had the sense of Bea. And it had that sense of Bea right there for you, so that you could feel it, you could sense the warmth of that message, you could feel the essence and really take it in. And you can, Bette, legitimately pursue your passion. (*Group repeats this again and again.*)

B: (*Whispering*) Thank you (*crying*).

I am sobbing now. My outer layer of insecurity gone, I am literally in Jeff's hands. He is holding my face and my tears pour into his hands. Part of me cannot believe this is happening and part of me is grateful as hell!

J: That was part of the ritual here. I know a good publisher so when will I get the manuscript?

B: (*Laughing and crying.*)

J: Now that we've already agreed to publish it.

B: I dedicated myself and raised my witness to doing what Harriet said of putting the grid into my life.

J: That's the central part of the book.

Central Part—Central Park. Brilliant, multilevel communication!

B: Yes, Yes, I would be remiss to say I'd have it done by the summer, but I'm going to have a good chunk. I have the proposal so I can commit to having the book with a proposal if you're so generous.

J: Yeah.

B: I've had that for a couple of years. I need some more vision because my style has morphed a bit since then. But I would love you to look at it.

J: Okay, that's great. Probably it's a popular book. It's something you want to have out to the trade, which is not really something that I can publish. I can't get things out into the trade.

B: It's more for lay people really but I want it to be something therapists can use too... what I'm writing is a developmental model for the integration of identity of single mothers. And I feel very passionate about that.

J: What's the concept of that? How do you go about doing identity?

B: Well, it's about wholeness. The title I have so far is Soul...playing on the word "soul" mothers. So, it incorporates meditation, spirituality of single motherhood as a path to uplifting and restoring the self to calling one into one's higher self. But the concepts in the model have to do with renegotiating the identity and consolidating the identity of the self in a new way.

Anchoring success: I am now integrating my wholeness, the wholeness of single mothers, I can make my book whole. Jeff has led me to my Self in many ways, and continues with genuine affirmations. I trust him totally now and, though a little bit of "I can't believe this is happening" is happening, I can take in his comments.

J: So, on the 14-point scale of being important, that ranks about 27.

B: For me and my work?

J: For me and my perspective of what needs to be done with people who get damaged and then they start to think of themselves as damaged people, which takes on an identity. And what you want to do is to help people to resurrect an essential identity.

Deep meaningful resonance with my wound, my passion, and the entrainment and connection I can have with the healing of others.

B: Absolutely.

J: So, that's huge.

B: And I'm using my story, which is very biographical. But I'm using my story in a way, and stories of other women, in a way to show I can do it, you can do it. We can do it together.

J: So, to whom would you tell the story to if you were using that methodology of putting a face on the screen and telling the story to [the face?] Would you tell the story to me, or would you reverse it and be me and tell the story to you?

B: I mean all of the above in some way. But I think… I would talk to… do you mean right now?

J: Oh, no. Yeah, that would be okay. We can do that.

B: I'm not sure of the context.

J: Well, I meant I'm imagining you at the computer and I'm imagining you being me at that moment. And I would imagine you being interested in why people, being interested in wiping the shit off of people's shame and helping them to…

Utilization perfection! Like Auntie Bea long ago wiping the shame from the shit, Jeff is wiping the shit from my soul. What a gift!

B: That's right. That's what it's about… wiping the shit…

J: So, at that moment you would use that energy of mishegass to channel me.

B: …and Auntie Bea would be beside me and she would say, "Bette, you can do it." And I would do it.

J: And you would be being Bea.

B: I would be being Bea.

J: To help a lot of people… I remember reading about Beatrice Wright, and Eric Wright was a famous figure in hypnosis when I was growing up…

In this next section, Jeff takes me more fully into another part of "central part," into another part of myself, into my passion and into my mission. I am still in trance. Both my conscious and unconscious mind are available to hear Jeff's affirming support, his many ways of integrating all I have told him and all I have experienced in the session.

He reframes my often disjointed relating of story into a metaphor of a wound in the process of healing. This effectively dismisses any last remnants of self-consciousness and shame about my being "spastic."

Jeff tells me about Eric Wright, a famous figure in hypnosis whose wife was a rehabilitation psychologist. This is information for my conscious mind, and nutrients for my unconscious mind to validate its own rehab process with spasms of healing that attend the giving up of the negative trance state and releasing its hold on my perception of myself. Toward the end of this important anecdote about the Wrights, Jeff affirms and implies an earlier collusion, which disabled and disconnected in some way my own ratification of my innate worth.

J: Rehab psychologist. She was one of the mothers of rehab psychology and the concept that she wrote was that there were people with a disability when the whole social system created an induction that you were a disabled person.

I am with him now on both information and unconscious absorption.

B: Oh, that is beautiful. (*More beautiful than my conscious mind knows.*)

J: And so once I got that concept in the 1970s, it has infused my understanding of how to help people with their identity when the induction of the whole social system is so great and people are stamped.

J: Give them the identity of being sole parent.

B: That's S-O-U-L.

J: Got it. (*Ratifying, again.*)

B: Thank you.

J: That's a great concept. Just reinforcing the necessity of having that concept out in the world in a way that will really inspire people. So, it doesn't matter, good enough or not good enough, or intelligent or not intelligent, it just doesn't matter. That's all superfluous. The essence of the matter is that you're passionate about this message.

Jeff goes on to validate the importance of my message to single mothers, the importance of my voice in the book.

J: And that you have an important message to bring out into the world. And what people are going to resonate with is your passion.

B: Thank you so much. When I'm in touch with that passion, the mishegass goes away.

J: Right. And if you started to entrap yourself into that mishegass, how do you channel us, or me...?

B: Well, I'm going to picture you and Auntie Bea and I'm going to do this... (*knocking on my head*).

J: Okay, and then you're going to stop doing that. And then just… (*putting his hands up to his face like blinders*).

B: I mean I can even just do this (*knocking on my head*) to remind myself not to do this (*moving fingers rapidly like typing*). Because this represents not doing this (*knocking on my head*) even if I'm not at a computer.

Now I've entered a more positive state, still a bit spastic, and it's okay.

J: Okay, how does that feel?

B: Feels really relieving. It's like I don't have to do that. I won't have to make myself… I don't have to put myself into a chained up place.

J: You were tethered, and it was a kind of peculiar age regression, particular age regression that you got into, and it was a swamp that you got into, and I'm just trying to beacon, including everybody, to have you (*puts hands to his face again like blinders*) focused on your passion.

B: I think part of what I'll do…I mean there are a number of things, but sitting here with you feels really like a gift, and sitting and being with this group and each individual is such a gift, I feel that I will take all of you with me. I get to take all of you with me. Thank you for being willing to come with me. And I'll just be in this room and feel here the loving support, the entrainment to my passion. It's just really the breathing that brings me back to the passion and I'm just so grateful. Thank you.

Now, putting it all together, utilizing all the messages including those from the group, Jeff helps me to re-associate the positive messages from Bea and from himself and from the group. He uses paraverbal communication, adding power to his words, to this central part of his therapy with his gestures.

J: Right. So here's passion; here's shame. If you do it this way…

B: The shame is on top.

J: It's reciprocal. So, if you get lost in the shame, you can't feel your passion. If you get lost in your passion, the shame will start to...

B: I'm going to use the image of cleaning up the shit.

J: For lots of people who really need that in the most poignant way.

B: So much. So much.

J: So, we're coaching you forward and you are picking up on the impetus. Right? So, now how do you want to... would it help you to build some accountability into this system?

B: It would scare me.

J: Yes. That wouldn't be good if it was too much, but a little bit of impetus might be okay. Accountability can be first that you send me the proposal.

B: That I can do because... but... I... oh see, I already have my "but."

J: But you stopped yourself.

B: Well, I owned the "but." I'll stop. I can send you the proposal, and I can be accountable to myself to carve out time this summer.

J: Okay. What's a reasonable amount of time that doesn't stress the system?

From here, Jeff negotiates my accountability for sending him my manuscript. By promising to send it to him, I commit to write.

J: Do you have a picture of her? (*Anchoring my commitment.*)

B: Oh, yes. I'll have her near me. I will do a meditation and remember that I promised to send it to you. I'll see everybody, feel their encouragement, and then I'll go to work.

J: And does that sound right?

B: Uh-hum.

J: Sounds eminently doable. Four hours?

B: It really does.

J: Even if you're writing yourself a check and putting it into your account—you're investing in yourself.

Now we discuss my work and my schedule, which at that point was grueling. Jeff suggests I pay myself for writing because he says I am investing in myself. This part went into the recesses of the unconscious, but I did send him the manuscript when I said I would.

B: I like that. That's really a wonderful idea.

J: Okay, I'm good. Are you good?

B: I am. I thank you so so much. It was really so wonderful.

J: The pleasure is mine.

Person: So, Bette, I don't know if you heard what Jeff's last words to you were and I thought they were important so I wanted to ask.

B: I heard words and I know they were affirming, but I'm in such a place, thank you Sue, I would love to hear them.

Person: Lo gusto es mio.

Person: You said, "The pleasure is mine."

B: Thank you, Jeff. I feel really privileged to have this time with you and with all of you.

Person: And we with you.

B: Thank you.

The Magic of Master Class

I chose to discuss my first NYC Master Class because it elegantly demonstrates the phenomenological nature of an Ericksonian approach, the artistry of Dr. Jeff Zeig, and the curative resources available in the Master Class itself.

Jeff welcomes me to the session with his posture and his gaze, and proceeds to utilize virtually everything I give him, as well as the dynamic of the group itself. He offers me therapy speaking to my conscious mind about rehabilitation while suggesting to my unconscious mind that I can believe in myself.

Throughout the session Jeff continues to ratify and utilize what I present, interspersing the idea of Central Park to achieve a deeper trance via destabilization and dissociation. He also utilizes the group's input first as a symbolic GPS and later as a chorus that increases destabilization, dissociation, and absorption. On the conscious level I think I am having a conversation about New York City and then about my book, but my unconscious mind is integrating a more central cohesive sense of Self.

The use of the metaphoric and interspersed idea of going to Central Park is intriguing. It adds the note of playfulness that Jeff has been witnessing as he has seen me "horsing around" with new friends during breaks. With playfulness and genuine kindness, Jeff is able to keep me untethered from negative trance throughout the session.

Does it come to Jeff intuitively to use Central Park as a metaphor? I believe that he is himself operating on both conscious and unconscious levels to be in a state of readiness to use all cues, overt and minimal. You may have noticed that there is no traditional induction in this session. This is not atypical of a session with Jeff in which the entire session essentially becomes the induction, the trance, the therapy, and the anchor. Rather than using a formulaic technique, Jeff is like an artist using a palette of conceptual and evocative communications to transform what the client serves up and to elicit a more positive Self-state. Affirming that I can remain untethered from negative trance, our session closes with Jeff as a compassionate and generous touchstone, reassuring me with kindness in his eyes that I can continue to believe that I am okay.

Additionally, you may find it interesting to observe the way in which curative factors of a group, such as universality, entrainment, and cohesion are revealed in this session. This is not an uncommon experience in our Master Class in which Jeff, and Helen Adrienne, hold us in high regard and authentic caring as we work to grow as therapists and as people.

From this day and many Master Classes forward, gifts will continue to be opened. My work will take on more depth and become more fun. Practicing psychotherapy, ready to utilize everything and anything, can virtually never be boring.

After much support and guidance from Jeff about finding a publisher, *Soul Mothers' Wisdom: Seven Insights for the Single Mother* is published (Pearlsong Press, 2015). And I have presented short courses at the Brief Therapy Conferences, and at the Erickson Congress.

Rick Miller

I attended my first New York City Master Class taught by Jeff Zeig over a decade ago. Walking into Helen's apartment was one of the scariest things I have ever done! New to hypnosis, I had chosen to be a novice in the Master Class. Working in front of people was hard enough, but doing Ericksonian hypnosis, which I knew nothing about, put me over the edge.

Fortunately, I made fast friends with the group. In my first session with Jeff, I focused on my usual complaints about working in a small town and struggling due to my lack of privacy—the same theme that continues to come up years later. Jeff brought me out of my contained stance quickly by having me enact running into clients in public. In front of the group, I had fun criticizing my clients for their imperfect outfits and drab shoes! The Master Class family got my number quickly, and Jeff facilitated my being able to come out of my shell perfectly.

The real anxiety, however, was about the therapy session the following day in which I was not the client but the therapist. After a sleepless night, I was as ready as I could be—adrenaline standing in for rest—to be Helen's therapist. Helen Adrienne always created a calm and welcoming atmosphere for newcomers, always attuned and generous. The session began, my heart was pounding, and Jeff instantaneously came to my rescue as Helen bounded into the room, dramatically jumping onto her chair. He sensed my terror and proceeded to "explain" something to the group, but I knew he was doing it for my benefit and I was grateful. We started again. I held my own, and I survived.

By the end of these first four days, the group had laughed together, cried together, joked about our Jewish heritage, and brushed up on our Yiddish since there were many members of my tribe in that group. I had never worked with a mentor like Jeff before—attuned, sensitive, expressive, yet complex with his indirect interventions. Even though I didn't know it yet, my destiny was about to unfold. My life has already changed behind my back! Jeff's exceptional gifts and the seamless synchronicity between him and Helen, combined with the complete acceptance of my new Master Class family, were a powerful draw and I was about to head down an entirely new path in their company.

Still, at the close of the first weekend, on the way to the airport and sharing a cab with Barbra Birge, a classmate, I said that I enjoyed the experience but that it was a little too expressive for me. I went on to assure Barbra that I probably wouldn't do another Master Class, and we parted. Of course, about a week later, I was writing to Jeff to say that since the class, something profound had happened to me that I couldn't even describe. "I slipped and fell into the (w) hole" is how I described it.

It is hard to communicate Jeff's impact in a concise way. Simply hovering together to deconstruct his interventions between sessions has an organizing effect on the group. Then, after Master Classes end, we stay in touch by various means to continue to process what we experienced together. Perhaps he isn't even fully aware of our ongoing attention to the work. The inspiration of the group experience lingers long after the group itself disbands.

Jeff's sincerity, caring, respect, and brilliance—his utilization skills and indirect interventions—are awe-inspiring. We all love him, and for good reason. It is an unusual gift to be able to win the respect of each student, leaving little or no room for competition among us. We are all well-fed and nurtured.

I have tried to figure out what it is about Jeff that creates this spaciousness into which each of our strengths is infused, while all of our vulnerabilities are accepted, and from which continually evolving wisdom is drawn. It must be his sincerity and warmth that are his greatest gifts. But this is only a tiny piece of the story. Over time, as I continue to extend my understanding of the complexity of the Ericksonian work, I find myself paying more attention, not less. Jeff's encyclopedic resources, which encompass various therapy modes, a thousand threads of poetry and music, innumerable acting metaphors and the utilization of all facets of life, form an extraordinary wellspring of topnotch therapeutic interventions. And this ever-expanding repertoire enables him to stay creative, attuned, and innovative. These moments together feel like life lines. We repeatedly enroll for the Master Classes. Some of us attend three times a year. It is an investment with exponential rewards.

On a more personal note, Jeff's acceptance of my being gay has been most healing. I feel his respect and his warmth always. This is an exceptional gift coming from a heterosexual male peer. He encouraged me to teach, endorsing me for big conferences all over the world, something I never imagined I would be able to do. He encouraged me to write, and then as Director of his publishing company, he offered me a contract for the book. Jeff—Dr. Zeig—has had the single greatest impact on my career of anyone. His confidence in me changed my life.

I also acknowledge that Jeff's generosity and boundless ability to connect—people, projects, concepts—are central to who he is as a person and as a professional. He has brought the psychotherapy world together as the architect of its central conferences in much the same way that he brings this Master Class together. As an individual, I am better for his presence; as a Master Class, we are blessed by it; as a professional community, we can only guess at the impact.

CHAPTER FOUR

A Moving Trance

Chanoch Rosenberg

As I set out to work on this project, I thought a lot about which of the many sessions to transcribe. I chose this one, because I find it to be truly a unique experience. Jeff and I go back a bit, and working on this project prompted me to reflect on our history together.

I first met Jeff when I attended his training in Israel in 1996. I was hooked immediately and have since attended numerous of his Master Classes. Each Master Class and encounter with him has contributed immensely to my growth and development as a therapist. Jeff often quips, and I cannot agree more, by now we are practically mishpacha, which is Hebrew for family.

There are certain key themes and concepts that Jeff uses throughout this session. The main themes include the use of utilization, confusion, and movement. Jeff applies utilization techniques often throughout. He utilizes my personality, religious background, playfulness, therapeutic style, and language as he is working with me.

Over time, I have come to anticipate and expect him to act in predictable ways. I therefore approach the session ready to go into trance, expecting him to be doing his usual, powerful routine. My expectation is that Jeff will hypnotize me, I will go into a trance, and then garner what I can out of the experience. Well, I am in for a big surprise. I am thrown off balance when Jeff suggests we change course, and that *I* hypnotize *him*. The tables are turned and instead of Jeff doing the work in trance on me, I am forced to take a more active role, one which I am not accustomed to. The session is not going to proceed as expected and this creates uncertainty and discomfort for me.

Metaphorically, or to use a metaphor I learned from Jeff, I am no longer grounded with both feet on the floor, I'm thrown off balance, and in order to regain equilibrium, I must keep moving and growing throughout the session. I am propelled out of my comfort zone, and since I don't know what is coming next, I can no longer stay passive. I am confused and therefore I am challenged to stay alert, focused and 'on my toes' throughout the session. The process of confusion prompts movement and growth; confusion leading to movement, the two of which are both vital ingredients to keep learning and growing. The discomfort and confusion I experience compels me to keep moving, moving forward towards an inimitable learning experience.

It is a moving trance, laying the seeds for and activating internal and external movement. It is a session with a message that includes a call for moving ahead and growing out of your comfort zone, awakening the guru within, all while still staying true to your unique integral self.

The Trance

J: Okay, Ready?

C: Set, go…

J: What do you have in mind to uh…?

C: (*Thinks.*) I would like to build up the idea of yesterday—

J: Okay?

C: —of the guru within…

J: Uh huh.

C: I would like to explore that more.

J: Okay, so how will that look?

C: Me going into a trance, and you doing your shtick… (*smiles.*)

Group: We can't hear, what did you say?

C: I said that I would be going into a trance, and he would be doing his shtick...

Group: (*Laughter.*)

J: Well... I would suggest an alternate route. (*Jeff is taking charge—and suggesting something different, something new.*)

And, what I would suggest, is, that you hypnotize me, to orient, eh, as if I were you, and you were orienting yourself to awakening the guru within. (*Now I am feeling off balance, he is making me work, think more. It also seems to me more playful.*)

C: So I should do the trance on you...?

J: Yes, but, I don't think your speaker is on... (*adjusting the volume.*) How is it now? Terrible... plug in equipment... how is it now? Better? Good? Okay.

C: (*Clears throat.*) So you want me to hypnotize you? (*I am confused, I am not sure if Jeff is being serious or playful, and I stay confused throughout.*)

J: Yes. (*Leans back, relaxes.*)

Pause.

C: Wonderful... and you know how to do it by yourself...

That's right...

going in even deeper... Discovering... who you really are...

and as you are nodding with you head... you can allow yourself to open up more...

(*Jeff seems responsive, yet I am still unsure if he is really in trance, or just playing along.*)

Opening, when you are breathing... so you open up, new... ideas ... Discovering... your significant way, of going into yourself...

and really appreciating who you are...

Sometimes, there is a fortune in your house and you don't even know that you have it... (*I was trying to use words to make him confident in himself. Jeff seeded the concept of the guru within, and I was using language to activate it.*)

Just by, turning around... and, taking in another deep breath...

Focusing, on the way your chest is rising... Up... and down...

Realizing... there is always more... than... you (*elaborating on the concept that you are bigger than your limitations.*) Know that you have... (*barking in background*) ...that's right... you could take it all in...

allowing yourself to drift even...

(*I am feeling lost, and waiting for Jeff to give me more feedback. Since he isn't doing so, I need to go on deeper.*)

You could let your mind... be here... and the other part be there...

Allowing yourself to discover...

Just like seeing that tip of the iceberg... knowing there is much more to that...

Appreciating... (*sound of machinery outside*) the noises... letting you know... there is much more there... than what you think there is.

Creating new holes... New openings... and allowing yourself... to remember... your past success...

Allowing yourself to appreciate... who you really are...

(*More barking.*)

That's right...

Remembering those moments... Allowing it... to define... yourself...

And all along... you could take that inner walk... visiting... different accomplishments... (*building yourself and defining yourself based on your successful moments*) one at a time... or altogether...

One part might listen... or another part remains searching...

(*I am prompting dissociation.*)

Going back... when you were younger (*here I am prompting age regression*). Different accomplishments... different struggles...

taking an easy breath...

And really see... that you have on whom to rely...

Really appreciating... what you thought is in others... you also have this strength...

Going back even more... even deeper... discovering... even more... those hidden assets...

That's right...

Allowing yourself... to take an even deeper, breath...

and to go in another deep level... seeing even the years before...

There has been... the foundation... the strengths...

the foundation of your wisdom...

and really... what you have learned from others, can become your own....

can become yours...

A strong pillar... to lean on...

and if you take an easy breath...

J: Help me to increase the strength and help me to activate and help me to orient into the future...?

I am not sure if he wants me to help him, or to help myself, and I am in a trance, trying to think. Do I have to hypnotize this master? or myself? and I have to go back to my inner resources.

C: And you can go back to yourself... revisit... the past... accomplishments...

Remembering... the struggles... the times that you wanted to give up... and you went forward... remembering the difficulties, the obstacles...

and how you utilized them... to get even stronger... to challenge your muscles... even more... even though your muscles were hurting... you knew it was growing pain... and you knew it's making you even stronger...

And just like when you drive your bike, it's difficult to go up a hill...

but you know that you can do it...

and you think how it's going to be once you reach that hill... how rewarding... it will be... how delightful you would feel...

and you know that you have the power... within yourself... you have the determination to do it...

so you could remember those hills...

looking into the future... one pedal at a time...

knowing... that you could make it... you have the power, that you have the ability...

Knowing the feeling of accomplishment... knowing the feeling... that you could do it for yourself...

It is nice to do it for others... you will gain even more if you could do it for yourself...

J: I have to switch gears... I have to stop doing one thing I am familiar with, in order to engage in something that is compelling to me.

C: ...and what is that?

J: Writing.

C: You want to stop to write?

J: No, I want to stop, seeing patients, which I am familiar with... in order to write.

Pause.

C: So you want to have... the feeling... I'm okay to do for others through writing... It's okay... to prioritize your writing, to seeing patients... You are doing a service... for others... and... you could balance out... time for writing... and time for seeing patients... knowing...

J: Stop, seeing patients?

C: Pardon?

J: Stop, seeing patients to write...? Stop what I've been doing, what I'm familiar with, to do something that is compelling...?

C: So you would want to stop seeing patients... so you could write all day...? And I could understand the insecurity feeling... that you might encounter...

However... you have... the strength within yourself... to know... that you could go on new ground...

You have the ability to develop... the struggle... and appreciate... your writing...

So you could be even more discovered, and bring out... your inner strength... your inner abilities...

J: Give me a moment...

C: Take all the time you need.

Long pause, 1.5 minutes.

C: Welcome back...

J: That was very deep... (*I feel that he is empowering me, he is giving me a compliment—feedback on the trance.*)

So the problem to solve is that, um, I have this grant to write

Erickson's biography... and, uh, it's a substantial grant, and in order to do that, and write the other things that I want, to write that, I have to stop doing what, I, have loved to do, and what's been really familiar to me, in order to do this.

So, when you were doing, that...

there were some idiosyncratic images—like, I was seeing an infinity sign... like a sort of flattened crater? And then it turned itself and, eh, it was the iceberg, and it was the depth of the iceberg that was coming, eh, up to the top.

And, um, your, your eh, components were excellent, really good. Because you covered all the bases, of dissociation, building responsiveness, increasing intensity, and focusing my attention, and so those things were really excellent and I appreciated them.

And then the metaphor of bicycle... (*I am still confused. He is giving me feedback that how I worked with him was good, but this should be my time for a session with him, so I am disoriented.*) ... and, eh, and you know, using my strength to get up the hill, was especially useful and then when I took the time, I was, um, organizing in my mind, some, uh, just like images, not a, not a, a plan, but it was like images, of how this would look, in the future. So that was great!

And, uh, I, can see that the, you know, I can feel, the immediate utility...

C: Keep me up to date, send me a postcard.

J: That what?

C: Keep me up to date, you will send me a postcard.

Laughter in the group.

J: Well, it's a really compelling, task and, uh, if uh,

if not now when... and if not me who... (*Jeff is utilizing my lan-*

guage, tailoring what he is saying to what I know of Biblical verses.)
…how does that go?

C: You said it right…

J: Okay, any questions? …No?

(*He is giving me supervision on what I could have done better, but I am still not sure.*)

I think that, uh, if you wanted to take that a step farther—so you could have certainly, uh, given me some sense of activity—and it would have been a metaphoric sense of activity—and it could have been, uh, imagining, uh, it could have been arm levitation, as an imagined activity, and it could have been something metaphoric, eh, seeing images, or, eh, even, feeling more intently the momentum of the bicycle, or seeing some, you know, maybe pinwheel image that was kind of a metaphor that spoke in parallel to the idea of activity. And, I liked the fact that you didn't do the inner guru in any direct way, that it was the components of the inner guru that you addressed, and that I could. You didn't have to mention it to me, because I could just keep it in mind and, um, then it was like feeding that inner wisdom or that inner guru, or the inner rabbi, or whatever you would want to call it. And… I wouldn't have wanted you to, um, connect the dots for me. I would, I could just, you know get the momentum of this, plus this, plus this equals seven—and that was very wise, that was a very, very good thing, that was very helpful…

I think that I was gone. (*He is describing the trance indicators.*) I was, I was in a different universe and totally lost track of my surroundings and what was happening around me, and that was great.

Sometimes your voice faded just a little bit, because of my, my bad hearing. (*Jeff is utilizing my trance, and in the feedback is also providing a summary of what a trance is all about.*) …but in the beginning your voice was really excellent, and then, maybe towards the end, your voice trailed just a little bit, and I had to

work a little bit to hear some of the things that you were saying and I know that being right eared, I know that I must have
turned my right ear towards you, I don't remember, and uh,
so that was something, eh, but there was something else, that
I can't even fully remember. Some metaphor about the house,
but I didn't, I only have some vague memory there, some amnesia there, I suppose that if I thought about it I could bring it
back, but that seemed to be really, eh, pertinent, so I'll just let
myself have the amnesia for it. And, uh, when I visited Erickson, my experience was that I would leave and then about an
hour later, poof, something would come back, and then later
that evening, poof, something would come back, and then a
day later, and then a week later, something would come back…
and that kept the momentum alive, and that was a really good
thing… and um, so, I think that, uh, it will help me a lot, and
it's really been a preoccupation about how I was going to create
a clear mind for myself and make sure that I was meeting my
promise to myself and not compromising to serve some greater
good, that wasn't really a greater good, that was only a fiction in
my mind.

And the greater good is served by doing what is compelling to
me right now. I can do it.

In order to do that, I have to divert from what was once very
familiar and rewarding to something that is now more compelling, and in order to do that I could see myself putting a sign on
the door that saying that by December 31, I will go on sabbat-
ical, and I don't know when exactly I will be back in practice,
and uh, then diverting referrals to other sources that I have, and
uh, then, you know, applying myself to the task at hand, which
is a little scary… a little daunting. I have two cartons, these
are not little cartons, these are two cartons of interviews that
I have conducted—and not all of them were even transcribed
yet. And then, I am going, at the end of this month, to Mena,
Arkansas, to visit Erickson's 85-year-old son, and, to Colombia,

Maryland, to visit his 75-year-old son, to continue to collect these interviews. I've been very good about these interviews. I have collected everything that I need, and more. And, uh, you know it could be an interesting diversion, an interesting distraction, to spend a lot of time on research. And my, um, my, the historical memory, was being a graduate student, cause you were stimulating the memory, right so, memories of successes. And I was seeing books, piles of books and I was thinking of the Evolution Conference and, uh, you know, the diligence and perseverance, and then the focus, in making sure that that happened. And, then I was back in graduate school, when I was a volunteer at a workshop, partly because they needed extra bodies for the workshop. And it was a writer and psychologist, and the workshop was on writer's block and the director, uh, said, "Writer's write, they don't research." He said if you wanted to write a book on whales migrating up and down the California coast, you write that, write that journal piece, write, and then you do the research. So, that was good to reinforce that in my mind, because it is easy for me to get lost in the research, and not draw the line, about being diligent, about writing, other people are shaking their heads, they know... (*laughter*).

So that was very good, that was very helpful.

So, I was listening closely, to what you were saying, and I was absorbing it, and I was absorbing it aggressively and actively and feel strengthened, empowered, and, uh, activated to go forth and do what it is that, uh, I have, uh, committed myself to do, and that is compelling to me, and serves a much greater good, when I really think about it, and I don't get lost in my own self-deception.

C: Wonderful!

J: Well, I think, we should do this more often...

Laughter.

C: Well, next week at, eh...

More laughter.

J: Okay, so uh, what, what do you think? What's your sense...?

C: About...?

J: Uh, I am returning to you, I had to, I uh... I was so self-preoccupied there... that uh... (*I think now that it may not necessarily have been about me all along. Jeff wanted a good trance, he had it, and he comes back to me now. Laughter.*)

I uh... okay... (*Jeff sits up and leans forward.*) Yup...?

C: I'm ready...

J: So, how do you resonate, with... what... you are about...

if I said to you in a deep, eh, hypnotic, em, trance that, um, comfort is overrated... (*I nod.*) And that, eh, pursuing, eh, the wrong master is a bit of a sin... (*Jeff is speaking my language again. I nod some more, Jeff pauses, reflects.*)

I can be so aggressive with these words...

(*Laughter.*)

But I will reciprocate cuz, eh, out of a sense of challenge, and a sense kindness, and appreciation!

So... begin, make yourself comfortable. (*Jeff is using hand gestures and movements of opening up.*)

(*I relax, lean back.*)

And realize... that you have your ways...

and recognize that you have your... approach...

Which leads you to your realizations... about how you can, let yourself...

be more open...

that's right...

so that you can allow yourself...

to rest... back.. comfortably and easily...

begin to recognize... the movement...

and realize the movement...

(*Jeff leaning forward, using left hand in flowing motion.*)

As you strengthen your sense... really strengthen your... growing sense...

of moving... more aggressively... assertively... into trance... (*Jeff is using motion and movement, both in language and actions.*)

And you can be as if you are thinking to yourself...

this I can assert... this I can do... this I can realize... (*He is feeding back my idea of "you can" and feeding it back to me with a twist.*)

And even the small movements, can somehow seem to change...

(*Jeff is expanding, spreading his arms wide with each "seem to change/evolve" statement.*)

And even the small movements can somehow seem to evolve...

As if... you are finding yourself... (*Again he is using my concept of discovery, and feeding it back, though differently.*) ...finding yourself... at home...

in a new realization...

finding within yourself... at home...

with a wealth... of memories... that strengthen.... your trance comfort...

and your conscious mind can be attending... and listening, to the movements... my movements, the movements around the room... (*Using movement and motion again.*)

While your inner mind, your unconscious mind... can explore...

explore the sense and the strength of the movements, within...

and in a curious way, there can be something that's uniquely comforting...

about the growing resolve... about the growing sense... about the evolving sense... the evolving resolve... (*Jeff uses triads and words with similar consonance throughout his work with me.*)

of being yourself...

(*Jeff opens his arms wide.*)

Even more... yourself... come to comfort... absorbed... in the experience...

of feeling that, realizing that, exploring that sense of movement,

and how, the movement... can be something... that you can... see behind your eyes...

and how the movement... can be something that you can feel in your body... (*I am a person who doesn't move a lot, I get the sense Jeff wants me to move ahead physically and metaphorically.*)

And how there can be memories... active memories that just dropped into place...

And how all along, the rhythms... of your breathing movements... change...

And how the movement of your hands... are different...

And how the sense... of your own... the movement of your own heart... beat... is different now...

(*My head is nodding forward.*)

And... the very wonderful sense of searching down (*he is utilizing my movement in trance and building on the theme of movement throughout*) inside yourself...

into a repository of memories, a repository of resources and accomplished realizations...

and just how you will develop your trances... in a way that

compels you in your life...

it may be something that... you take the time... to search down inside of yourself...

enjoy the images... enjoy the sensations, realize the perceptions... (*Utilization of my words, with the emphasis for me to keep moving in my unique way.*)

...in a way that is uniquely you...

annnnd...

curiously... there can be an even more expanding sense...

(*Jeff opens arms wide repeatedly here.*)

and I don't know just how you can recognize... how you can realize, expanding sense... in a way that is compelling...

and the way in which your right hand, is moved into a different position...

how there can be a different sense of strength...

and what's interesting now? What are you exploring, experiencing now...?

(*Jeff wants to check in where I am holding back. He is not okay with it being a simple relaxed trance. He wants to deepen the experience to make it more active. I pause, thinking in trance.*)

C: General positive feeling...

J: And it is so nice to sense... and feel and... memorize...

Because those are sensations, those are feelings, those are perceptions, to which you can return...

Finding yourself, again, again and again, and again... (*Upon reflection, I am aware that Jeff hardly says a word, or offers a sentence, without using his hands.*)

...more vibrantly...

absorbed in the experience...

What else are you experiencing now…? What else are you exploring…?

Long pause.

C: The comfort.

J: Yes,

and the way in which it can feel to you, as though somehow, curiously, your moving… forward…

A sense that you are bringing forward…

(*Again, he is using hand movements with each "forward word" and "expanding word."*)

And inspiring…. sense…

an inspiring repertoire…

Expanding…

In ways that… represent… your growth, that represent your style, that represent your wisdom…

And is it okay to awaken yourself, with a compelling sense of… moving forward…

Really okay…

Really strong…

And take as much time as is right for you…

To take one, or two, or three easy breaths… and bring yourself back… fully alert and rested… and refreshed… wide awake…

Hi, what was that like?

C: Wonderful.

J: Really wonderful?

C: Cholent!

J: Huh? What's that?

C: A good dish.

J: Aha, and help me to understand some of the things that were going on with you.

C: I don't know how much I was... here... just in general, I don't know, good.

J: And, okay, you could know if you pushed yourself to know, so there's something about not knowing that's immediately compelling...?

Which is, my projection, so that is just be with the experience and not explore or try to understand, just allow the Experience like a seed—

C: Right.

J: —to fertilize inside you.

C: Right.

J: And see what momentum it has.

C: That's right, and I guess we'll listen again....

J: ....of course you can email it to me, and I can listen to it again... (*Again, Jeff is utilizing here. Laughter.*)

I'm serious...

All right, is that good...? Is that spirited...?

C: (*Nods.*)

Summary—utilization, movement, triads, body language.

J: Okay, thank you so much!

Comment

As you can see from the session, it begins with me requesting an elaboration on the concept of "the guru within." Jeff allows me that experience via an unexpected route. By being challenged to hypnotize the master, I am given an opportunity to not only find my guru within, but to share its wisdom with others, a very empowering and moving experience throughout. Jeff's use of utilization, augmented by confusion and movement, highlight both my playful side, as well as my tendency to be more passive in trance. I am left with much food for thought after this amazing experience, which compels me to continue to challenge myself both in my personal and professional life.

CHAPTER FIVE

My Stroke, a Stroke of Luck, and My Wise Advisor

Susan Dowell

S: I have been really looking forward to talking with you. Lots of things have been happening. I went to Bremen to teach at ISH this summer and I had a really unsettling experience. I was looking forward to doing some sightseeing and got there a few days before my presentation. I woke up early the next day, wanting to write some additional thoughts for the presentation, before I went out. But to my horror, my right hand was paralyzed. I couldn't even grasp my pen. In fact, I could not move my whole lower arm at all.

I thought I was having a TIA, and the doctor told me when I got back to NYC that it was a stroke.

J: Oh, and now no residual?

S: No there are no residuals in my hand or arm, but nonetheless, I probably should have gone to the hospital. But I spontaneously went into a trance and remembered reading, in a science magazine, that if you had that kind of stroke, it was important to get the arm and hand moving as soon as possible.

So I stayed in my room, did visualizations that blood was flowing back and forth through my brain, and simultaneously doing arm and hand exercises using my left hand to move my right one. I just stayed focused on keeping my arm and hand in motion, until I could feel my arm moving on its own volition. It took a number of hours, but my arm and hand were fine after that, for the rest of the trip.

But then, when I got back to New York, I noticed a flutter in one eye. And I realized I was being too glib and I needed to take this more seriously. I figured it was time see my neurologist. He gave me a big battery of tests, an MRI on my chest and my brain... and he told me, I had several blood clots from my accident a few months earlier. He also told me that since the paralysis in my hand lasted more than 4 hours, it was definitely a stroke that I had while I was in Germany.

So now I am on Coumadin every day and I've changed my diet, since I can't have many foods with a lot of Vitamin K. And I'm going regularly to the PT. Physically I feel better than I have in years but I am very shook up!

J: And other things, circulatory issues?

S: Coumadin and diet and exercise are the most important to deal with this. I have to be... rigorous about following through.

J: So, you are taking care good of yourself.

S: Yes, I feel better physically and I am feeling very relieved about that. But there is one other issue or maybe it is part of the same issue. There are times when my memory is not what it should be—very unsettling. I keep a lot more notes than I used to just to be sure. But it's very unsettling and I am hard on myself. I want to stop being so hard on myself. I double-booked a new patient last week by mistake. Those things happen, but he made it into quite a drama. This new patient, who was double-booked, yelled at my other patient. Even though I tried to intervene, I was a little flustered, especially by his outlandish behavior... and also annoyed at myself for letting this happen and it got in the way of my taking control of my own authority, much like I felt when I was a kid. "How could I do this?" Things were always blown out of proportion by my mother. That is what I call my, "Uh-oh feeling."

J: Let me tell you a story. Carl Whitaker was an impactful influence on me. I remember when Whitaker screwed up and had more than one patient on his schedule he would bring them in and see them at the same time. So that uh-oh is just a check. Just an alarm. The purpose of the alarm is to alert you. (*Jeff pauses and looks at S's posture.*)

J: When you are in that posture, with your head down...

S: This posture starts the story. The old challenge—I did it wrong. I'm ashamed... It disempowers me. I'd like to put it on that shelf.

J: Suddenly you are back into that old story. Like a seizure of shame. How is the recovery? Is it like this, or this, or this? (*He demonstrates with his arms. Holds one arm rigidly with other hand.*) So something you can remind yourself of is breathe in the now, like Helen would do, breathe in the moment.

S: I do. I pull myself out, but then...

J: You pull yourself out, but it is a struggle.

Yes, and that may take a little bit of time, a little bit of doing to get yourself in place. Let's just assume that this (*arm gesture*) is inevitable. Just cavalierly assume this is inevitable. It will happen today, it will happen tomorrow, with a patient, or whatever you are doing, this is in place. It is inevitable. Let's make it happen in this moment. I would say something about keeping your chin level and your face level.

So take a moment and orient yourself and recognize some of the steps that you take that you recognize to get to that trance-forming state where you are safe to explore inside and recognize the capacity to guide you in ways that are pleasant for you and to know that you are forming new connections and new minds in your brain and you are feeling at ease inside yourself in ways that are important and that are really memorable.

Like there were moments when I was with Erickson and suddenly in a flash I am back in Phoenix and he is leaning forward and smiling and suddenly there is a sense that everything is

right. At the recent brief therapy conference I was with Paul…
and he spent many hours with the Dalai Lama. He was writing a
book on experiencing anger in irrational places and he was with
the Dalai Lama and suddenly he realized, "I am in the presence
of goodness," and he was asking the Dalai Lama, "What did
you do and how did you do that?" and the Dalai Lama said, "Of
course…". And I don't know what you can do in your mind to
rearrange what is physical and what is mental and even physiological and the way that that uplifting spirit begins to infuse your
experience so that you can feel that moment where re-storying
something is an ascendant experience. And the way in which
you feel that your shoulders lift and breathe. A moment of an
ascendant experience and as you deepen and intensify this entrancing moment, you give yourself time to work yourself into
it to feel yourself into it, to effortlessly experience it even more.
And as you do that, where do you find yourself now?

S: I went back in time to be with that younger me. I gave her what
she didn't have at that moment, which is an embrace, and I took
her hand and went like this (*S. rubs her hand—J. rubs her hand.*)

J: What's it like in your heart?

S: I feel like I connect to the loving… and the troubling turmoil,
which was part of my parents' perspective that they passed on
to me. Back and forth. It's like the wall between (1) this is me,
feeling loved, and (2) this is me feeling criticized. It's perme-
able.

J: It's like you can have a seizure of shame, you can have a seizure of
hope, a seizure of connection…

S: It's like I was a little kid. I need to stop dwelling on the inconsis-
tencies and aloneness of childhood, and I need to bring myself
into the present moment.

J: So, as you feel that old shame attack in your body and hold it for
a minute, you can begin to recognize that you can begin to feel
the strength from that, so it begins to become you, and it real-

ly becomes you in so many senses and then there's a moment when you let go and you begin to resurrect a new way, a new way of being and a new way of understanding, a different way of being!

S: There's a piece that is important. I realize the mistake I had made, I realized that this woman was very upset when I called her. I realized I had put her in that situation. She didn't want a repair from me. I apologized to her, she didn't want anything to do with me anymore so I couldn't repair it with her. I couldn't resolve it in the context of the situation so I had to forgive myself. I think it was a little harder.

J: And then, as you are more like this, and more like this and more like this… (*Uses his hands.*)

S: You know, I never in those moments as a child had someone who would come to me and say, "You know, it is really okay. You didn't mean it, you can't repair it, and it is still going to be okay."

J: Okay. Think whatever steps you know from your experience, and you know from the heartland, it is not just words.

S: (*Embraces herself with her arms hugging her chest.*)

J: Nice, so take some time with that. And what is happening now?

S: That's the piece I think I was reaching for. It's about moments that are irreparable that I have to forgive myself for and not go into a downward spiral about. Everyone has those moments.

J: It was nice to watch some of those old movies. And how they would always wind their way to a satisfying ending. And then the title would flash in some kind of script: The End. And then you would go to the next episode.

S: That's what I'm feeling in my life now.

J: Fantastic. And you are following the prescription and doing all of the things that you know how to do to strengthen yourself. And that is an awesome experience. And what's happening now?

S: I was playing with the word, awe, aw-shucks. Don't know where that came from. I'd like to find some way to anchor it just a little bit more so it's there.

J: Okay, so if you were choosing a color for embedding it a little bit more, what color would you choose?

S: Rose red.

J: So, as you take that color and generate it in your mind, what pattern would you create for that color?

S: I see rose petals.

J: And what would you want to do in relation to those rose petals?

S: I see my relation to them and the texture of them and...

J: And as you relax into that awesome universal state of just smelling and feeling and realizing and then there could be memories that further empower that experience, and knowing that in this moment you can think back with that sense of strength as you can look forward to the continuation of that sense. And embrace it. In a way that is personably yours.

S: (*Takes in a deep breath.*)

J: What is happening now?

S: I had an image of being enveloped by both things. I find it regenerative to feel like I am waiting for myself (*opens arms outward*), it feels so empowering.

J: It doesn't need a word. It just needs a felt sense.

S: I hope that having that image is really very special.

J: What is happening now?

S: I feel power in my arms and now that I am working out I feel much more of this.

J: What do you feel you need right now to put an end to this session. What would cap it for you?

S: I feel like humor...

I am really looking forward to an experiment. My husband

would say I look forward to ways to get past each obstacle. I feel like this challenge, um, one of the gifts my mother gave me without realizing it. She would say, when I wouldn't listen to her, "You don't take no for an answer." I think that is who I am today. It feels like my companion. Those words are my companion as I move forward with things.

J: Yeah. Embrace them!

S: And with my "Footprintings" work I am using them as a pattern to get through this too.

J: I encourage you to have a crisp and satisfying ending to this session.

S: I have an image of me taking your hand and walking forward. I don't know where I am going. But that's all right, I feel safe with it. Being in the mist...

J: So, bring yourself back. Very good work. Pleasure. Good to work with good people. So, we can end with a hug? Normally I wait for the other person to offer but not in this case. (*End in embrace.*)

Comments

This was a momentous session. It is now five years later, and I remember it well, and I learn even more from it as I reread it. Jeff has a remarkable way of being supportive, gentle, curious, confronting, creative, and open—all at the same time, in a way that makes everything feel safe. This session occurred at a particularly difficult period in my life when I was undergoing a number of personal transitions, and rereading the session for this book has revivified my learning and expanded my perspective, once again.

Jeff also, so often, has a story that matches my concerns or problem. It is remarkable to me how he does that. And that gives wings and shape to my learning as I see more and more permutations and options to use it. So much easier to absorb insights from that perspective, so much easier to move forward.

I have highlighted particular sections that touched me as I went back over this 2012 session. But who knows, the next time I read it through, I might connect to something else. That is what is so special about Jeff's "universal wisdom."

Sara Millstein

I have been a participant in Master Class at least once a year for about 10 years... learning the power of words, the impact of a story and a metaphor... the power of a group of people who come together first as professionals and then become family.

One sunny spring Saturday I was staying in a small town in upstate New York, and had the job of taking the garbage from home to the recycling center. This is not something that someone who grew up in NYC experiences. I threw the garbage in the back seat of my little Honda. When I arrived at the recycling center I parked and surveyed the scene trying to figure out where each category of trash went. I was surrounded by pick-up trucks, dump trucks, and commercial garbage haulers, and my thought was me and my little Honda completely didn't fit in. I felt really uncomfortable. I figured it out the best I could, and then jumped back in my car and searched for the exit.

I then went to the farmers' market where I felt at ease and began to think about the experience I just had and how that feeling of not fitting in might be a theme for me and how the story could be used with patients who feel they don't fit in.

In November 2013 I was unsure whether or not I should keep my place at Master Class. I had just finished chemotherapy. Would I be able to participate in the wonderful process that is the Master Class, would I take away from other people's experience? I debated and debated. I called Helen the night before class was to start and told her I wanted to come but might have some extras needs. And with no further discussion, I appeared the next morning to take my place. As soon as I arrived I knew I had made the right decision; there was no discomfort. I was treated as one of the family. I participated and felt a wonderful sense that I was not the experience I had just been through, but a professional, who had something to offer, and a valued member of a family. I was shocked that I had made it through the four-day class. This would not have been possible except for the exceptional people who participate in it. They are not simply outstanding therapists, they are extraordinary people.

I once again discovered that I had a place!

CHAPTER SIX

Traveling Together

Wei-Kai Hung

J: So, where will you have us arrive, and how do you want to travel?

Starting from the beginning, Jeff sets the tone for this session. He uses the words "arrive" and "travel" to imply that this will be a journey. He uses the word "us," not "you," which implies that this will be a journey we take together. He implies that he is interested in learning where I want to travel. This is spoken in a tone of curiosity and from there, I feel safe and become curious about where I want to travel and what I want to explore during my journey. In other words, I will be the tour guide, and he will follow. This is a short opening, yet within it, there are multiple meanings, including curiosity, warmth, welcoming, caring, and an implication that he is genuinely interested.

W: Thank you for saying that. So I'd like to start this day with gratitude, especially the appreciation, the appreciation for you.

Three years ago when I went back to Taiwan, I did not know what to do, where to start with everything.

J: You did your internship and study here?

W: I studied here and worked here, and I just quit everything and went back to Taiwan. And I met you there in Taiwan, and since then, the journey has been wonderful. And I just woke up and it is dream come true. I need to give you a hug. Just like Father Jim did yesterday.

J: Father Jeff (*a parallel joke*).

W: I woke up, feel okay, and here I am right now. So where do I want to go? That really is the question you are asking me and I am asking myself. Especially turning 40. Once again Helen reminded me this morning about that.

J: Isn't that special in the United States for that number, and in China the special number will be 36 or 48. Which is much more significant?

When I talk about my age, I am worried about reaching age 40, which is considered middle life. I also thought about the mid-life crisis. Jeff quickly points out the cultural difference, which is not only a distraction from my mid-life crisis concern, but also a really important issue that puts me back into a different perspective. He is aware that American culture and Chinese culture have different perspectives about numbers and ages. For example, in Chinese culture, numbers such as 12, 24, 36, and 48 are meaningful and considered good numbers. In Western culture, 10, 20, 30, 40 are considered meaningful with regard to different stages of the lifespan. I am deeply influenced by both cultures, and here I decide to use a Western viewpoint to see my mid-life crisis. Turning 40 years old bothers me, and I want to review my past 40 years, and plan my future 40 years.

W: You are right, it's different meaning. Yes, there are couple things I'd like to make out. I really don't know what to do this year. There are many things going on right now in my life, and I want to have an archetype or anchor for myself. I want to go into the unknown zone and experience a new state. Because last year I remember you and Chanoch helped me go through a wonderful year and I accomplished a lot of things I never dreamed of. So, this year I want to have a gift for myself.

J: Sure, and would a way of traveling be to do that with trance? And a way to do the trance is immediately let yourself sit back, and can you take a moment to feel what it is like to sit back, to explore. What it is like to sit back. And you can notice something else to do is to be... be aware of your breathing and how sitting back provides supports... and how you support yourself with air and then as you continue into trance you may notice the way in which... in which things slow down and somehow as time seems to change (*he speaks more slowly*) that also is a way of supporting yourself as you go into trance and you may notice that there are other things that also change and there is part of the adventure of going into trance and how some senses can seem so acutely attuned (*spoken smoothly*) like you can be acutely attuned to the tone, acutely attuned to the tempo, acutely attuned to the meter, to the rhythm of my voice and how you no longer need to pay attention to the way in which your breathing rhythm has slowed down and you no longer need to pay attention to the way which time, it can change, seems so often unimportant. And how each time you go into trance it can be a way in which you adventure, a way in which you explore, and be delighted by the realization that you discover.

After a few minutes of talking, Jeff does not hesitate to jump in to create a trance as a departure for our journey together. I am so curious about how he knew when it was the right time to start the journey. I find two interesting things here. First, his opening line in this session is about discovering my journey, and that is exactly what's in my mind before the session begins. I feel as though he can read my mind, and I was surprised. I give him a few cues, the issue seems very big and vague. He catches the cues and gives me back some hints/suggestions that are proved to be accurate and important in the later part of this session. Second, from the beginning Jeff shows me how much he trusts me as he guides me into a trance right away to explore more. When I conduct hypnotherapy sessions with others, more information is needed, and I need a longer time to make sure clients are ready for hypnotherapy. Once again, his actions show me multiple meanings, including that he trusts me; he knows I am ready to go into trance; he is willing to follow my footsteps on this journey. I tend to believe that he receives many minimal cues from my body language, and all these minimal cues tell him that I am good to go. In order to reach that detail-oriented conclusion, he and I both need to be in a concentrated and relaxed state. Simply put, we both need to be "in the zone," and communicate in the zone state. When my body realizes he is jumping into action and how much he trusts me, I feel that he builds a safe and secure field for both of us. I do not care what's happening outside, and I only want to enjoy our journey together. In other words, I am excited and ready to go! By the way, to go on a journey in a trance, we first need to build a trustworthy and safe environment because an unknown journey may be risky and dangerous; nobody knows if it will be a positive or negative trance journey. In the next part, we can see even more clearly how Jeff utilizes my body language in a positive way. We can also see some tailoring techniques.

J: For example, although you consciously allow yourself to easily, easily sit here, it may feel to you as though somehow you are moving forward, it may seem to you somehow, it suddenly feels as somehow a path begins to open. It may seem to you almost as if there is a compelling force that begins to draw you forward, so that you can rest back into the support and curiously realize there are compelling senses that can suddenly focus the adventure of going into trance, and how there can be a deepening sense of exploring, and finding some realizations that guide you in your journey to realize trance, realize trance just for you, and to notice how some things can be really uplifting and other things can just stay right in place (*arm levitation, in which my arm lifted on its own*), and the way in which somehow that uplifting realization can somehow happen in a series of steps. And that there is a step, a step-wise realization, almost as if there has to be a compelling curious compelling sense that has you realize that there are some things that are really previously left behind but that are now somehow much more alive and much more uplifting. And that sense, that uplifting sense can continue and even begin to develop a curious, a curious momentum. And your conscious mind could attend to the warmth of the room and your conscious mind could attend to your own sense of gratitude, about that journey and the way in which that journey begins to change, and there's a momentum in which that journey is different (*his pace speeds up*) and how there can be a trajectory that you may not know consciously. For example, the way in which your hand in that stiff right way lifts up toward your face (*my arm kept lifting and was ready to touch my face, although I did not know how it would touch my face*). Almost as if there is something about your mind that draws that to an unknown place consciously... and your conscious mind may not know where your hand can touch your face, and my conscious mind can't really know just where that hand can touch your face. And your unconscious mind can really know as if unbeknownst to you consciously your inner mind has already decided and the way in which your head moves, different kind of movement, more of unconsciously right movement, and the way other things just drop away so that the left hand lifts, the right hand follows and all along, all along you are exploring the capacity of your inner mind to guide you. And the way in which there can be that compelling sense of your hand finding its own rhythm to lift up and touch your face, knowing, realizing when that hand touches your face, that can be a signal, with your eyes closed, and looking up to the top of your head, and finding an easy breath, and to know that that helps you even more, to be more intuitively involved with the exploration... of your trance, in your way. And taking time to explore and to feel and to sense and to realize how things can just seem so right. And even though there may be some sense of disorientation, not knowing exactly where your hand is in space, you can trust the trajectory, the movement of your hand, that your hand knows just what's right for you. Exploring easily, exploring fully, allowing adventure to develop itself. And you know the experience of walking on a summer's day, a gentle rain, and how pleasant it can be to experience the moisture in the air. Almost. Almost. Almost. (*My hand is about to touch my forehead—the image of the telescope eye in the forehead, the third eye position, and ready to see through my future.*)

In this paragraph, Jeff synchronizes his breathing with mine, and closely observes my minimal body movement. He conducts a trance and monitors my body movement with keen eyes. I feel he knows what my body wants to move next, and it is as if he has a pair of X-ray eyes seeing through all my inner voice and thoughts, and understands what my unconscious wants to do. I feel very good to be understood from inside. A Chinese saying is appropriate here: I feel that he is the bug that stays inside my stomach, he knows everything about me. I trust him, and I know my minimal body movement and behaviors are perceived and understood in a deep respectful way. I realize that I do not need to open my mouth to talk and he would follow these minimal cues from my unconscious on this journey. The trance process becomes so easy that my conscious mind and his eyes were together in observing how my unconscious body moves itself, and everything Jeff says is a plus, nothing stopping me from going forward. Jeff uses beautiful, musical-like hypnotic language, leaving me amazed by every sentence he speaks. I deeply enjoy the trance and his musical poetic language, and it certainly feels like he is inside my mind traveling with me. We were traveling partners. Jeff follows my body movements and feeds them back to me as a tool to deepen my unconscious journey. In the previous section, he trusts my conscious mind to initiate the journey, and now he further trusts my unconscious mind to guide us through this journey deeper and deeper.

J: (*Deep breath.*) That's right. And I remember asking Dr. Erickson to autograph a book for me and he wrote: "One of the wonders of the world is the opening of the eyes." And certainly in Western culture we know about having two eyes (*the third eye*). And how there maybe intuitively a realization of a deeper sense and more profound way of seeing and how your head is effortlessly turned to the right and how it can seem to you as if you're looking through a telescope, so that you can further focus your vision and explore an adventure now. I can certainly remember in some of my earlier days using Erickson as a mirror, as a model, and certainly in my formative days it was easy to think, "What would Erickson advise? What would Erickson do?" And that was a wonderful kind of alchemical sense of an archetype that could serve as a temporary way of envisioning understanding, responding (*I saw a pyramid with my third eye*). And that as you begin to realize your perspective, your adventure, your exploration, your way of traveling, then gently your left arm can move back down. So it can com…com…com…comfortably rest.

Jeff starts telling a small story about Erickson, and as he speaks, it is clear that I am very interested and will listen carefully. The words "wonders" and "eyes" are like a pebble dropped deep into my unconscious pond, splash, and many ripples spread out. He sees my hand movement and he immediately uses it to describe the telescope in the trance induction. At this particular moment, I am lifting my left hand slowly to reach my forehead, the third eye position (I did not tell him my image of the telescope during the trance). As soon as he points out the telescope image, I know that it is right, and that is exactly my image of lifting my left hand to touch my forehead. There is a telescope in front of my third eye. I realize at this point, I can allow myself go anywhere I want to go, and share with him about my inner images later. Then Jeff adds some minimal elements into my trance; it is about my favorite concepts regarding alchemy and archetype. I am surprised that he remembers my mentioning this briefly in our initial conversation. I am happy that he listens and remembers what I said, and uses it perfectly with the right timing. Near the end of this paragraph, he starts using "com…com…com… comfortably," and this repeating word with an emphasis on "com…" has a double meaning to me. It is an invitation to enjoy the comfortable feeling, and it also sounds like calm, come deeper. A simple word within the trance can provide some interesting associations and meanings. This singing-like sentence brings me into deeper trance.

J: And find a position, find a place that really is right for you, comfortably for you so that you can be more confident in the capacity of your own mind (*my left hand moved aside open*), and the way in which the time… is so interesting, and the way in which orientations can suddenly change, the way in which you can allow yourself to reach forward into realities that are meaningful for you (*I opened my palm*). And the important thing is for you to understand what your hand is saying to you, and understand the feelings of your hand, the orientation of your hand, and the expression of your hand and meaning of that expression for you, and almost as if there's a wisdom in your hand. It can delight you, it can surprise you, and increase the sense of the story, focusing. Then something else that you may enjoy, something else that you may delight in experiencing, maintaining the trance in the body of your experience. You can open your eyes and reorient yourself from the neck up. And that can be a very interesting experience, the way in which the focus of your eye can be different. The way in which your eyes blinking, in which the colors, the shapes of your eyes can be different. What's it like? What is meaningful to you?

Jeff leads me into deeper trance, and during this period I am keenly aware of my left hand moving in a horizontal direction. It is an interesting experience for me to be aware of several images at the same time while my hand moves outward horizontally. Jeff realizes that I am in a deep trance and seem to be discovering some interesting images. He decides to invite me to reorient and brings me back to discuss what I see and how I feel. During this period of time, there are three things that occur simultaneously: (1) My hand moves on its own. (2) Some inner images appear. (3) My body goes more deeply into trance while I open my eyes and speak from my observing, conscious mind.

W: I've seen the path, when you said the path, walking toward the direction. In the beginning it was just some holes, nothing there. And then I found something in my third eye, I found a telescope to look through, and I see. I kind of adjust the telescope.

J: Adjust the telescope so you can really see more in a focused way, and yes~

When Jeff speaks about the telescope, vision, and focus, immediately vivid images pop up and I can describe them through my conscious mind. He said, "yes" with a windy lingering sound at the end of the sentence. This helps me to look thoroughly into these inner images and become even more relaxed. I feel that Jeff sends out another invitation to share my discovery with him.

W: I see a golden colored mountain when I hear your voice, and I turn to you (my head, my hands, and the left side of my body), and I see your entity, just kind of all different kinds of colors. It's like a rainbow color.

J: A rainbow color?

W: Yes, like red, yellow, purple.

J: And am I on the mountain?

W: It's different. Mountain is there, and you are here. Sometimes they collapse together. The golden color is shiny.

J: The golden color is shiny and some collapse between the gold color and the mountain and me and the path?

Here Jeff is in essence repeating what I just said. This serves two purposes. First, when he repeats these sentences in his own way, it enhances these images and strengthens my connection to these images. Second, his repeating sentence allows me to see images from a more detailed perspective; therefore I can explore deeper meanings within this journey. I know I very much enjoy this journey. It feels good that someone really listens and repeats it back to me. Not only does he not miss any important word, but also he uses his own tone, voice, and style to feed it back to me. It feels like hearing echoes between mountains or at the bottom of a mountain valley.

W: Yes. And I looked further into the path, and I see people I love, people who love me, they are cheering for me at the end of road, and waiting for me to go there, so I feel happy.

J: Because there is strength, there are people who love you, they are there cheering for you in the path?

W: Yes, and then an amazing thing happened when you told me to put the hand down. When my hand was on the way back to my lap, I feel that—(*Jeff turns his hand*)—yes. A flower, a bunch of flowers on the side of the road. Very beautiful, also very comfortable.

We both are enjoying the journey now; whatever Jeff is doing will signify my thoughts and feelings. To be more accurate, I feel like looking into a mirror at this moment. He turns his palm up, and I feel something start changing inside my body.

J: What kind of flower?

W: Just one flower, the name came up, a mayflower. I found it's interesting. It's a mayflower, I don't know if it makes sense or not, it's just mayflower. And mayflower has many colors. I remembered purple.

J: Purple is a very good sign around here.

Everyone laughs because Erickson could only see purple, and we all are Milton Erickson's students, and we know the story of purple well. Therefore, purple is meaningful to me and to Jeff as well. Jeff is playful and I enjoy his humor.

W: Yes. Along with other colors.

J: And there was something else that happened. What was the meaning of that?

W: You are right. There is a sentence: "Let love in." So that is meaningful to me.

J: Say it again.

Jeff does not continue talking about purple. He senses something is hap-

pening within me, and he is right. I see other things with the eye of the heart, my inner eye. The words "let love in" suddenly appear. This short sentence just slips out of my mouth and my conscious mind is surprised by what just happened. Jeff senses that this sentence is very important and meaningful to me. He encourages me to say it again and really experience it more deeply. Jeff does not know that before he encourages me to say it, I have already said it over and over again quietly. Jeff and I both know that to whisper inside my heart and say it out loud will be totally different experiences.

W: Let Love In (*together with Jeff*). It just appeared a few times. It came from the bottom of something. It hits me, I don't know. Let Love In.

This is the part where I feel amazed. I do not know how or when he decides to start another trance. I know inside my mind that it is the right timing to begin another trance, and I only become aware of that after the second time I say, "let love in." When Jeff says the sentence with me, the synchronized voice and tone triggers a strong sensation. Although I do not know what it is, it feels like an ocean current or a stream of force/ energy. I realize that when I said the bottom of something it means the bottom of my trunk, and the inner voice of "let love in" comes from it, and it is a perfect time to go on with another trance.

J: Brilliant. Allow yourself to gently close your eyes. And allow yourself to easily, peacefully meditate on "let love in." And you can take a moment. An unadulterated moment. And that's a curious art, take an unadulterated moment. And experience in your way what an unadulterated moment can be. And that as you take that unadulterated moment, what could follow sequentially, is a sense of gratitude. About your own inner mind, and trajectory, adventure, and you can take in sequentially, orienting to the mayflower, orienting to the love, and it can be so nice to take this moment, to feel, to experience and explore, in the gratitude of your own mind, those two experiences, and continuing in this unadulterated moment, and the next step is to realize the meaning of that, let love in, and take in a way that may or may not make any sense consciously and the next step could be that once you find that meaning you can woo that meaning as if there is something that is a felt sense in your body. And you can move let love in, that as the felt sense you can feel the shape, the texture, the sense, the physicalized sense in your hands, and that you can have the sensation of "let love in" in the back of your hand. So that you can grasp it, and hold it, and sense it. And that you could realize as a sensation the meaning of "let love in" in the heart of your experience (*my hands reach my heart*) and breathe new life into it. And that you can even sense "let love in" in your abdomen. Now, in a Western metaphor, when you have something in your abdomen, something in your gut, the meaning of this is something fitting, this is something I deserve. And a Western person is thinking that this is something I have a gut feeling for, this is something I deserve.

Jeff artfully uses voice and tone to direct me into my own direction. This is the time for integration. I express my gratitude, and integrate "let love in" and the mayflower. Jeff's timing in closing the loop amazes me. Once again, he accurately speaks my mind regarding when and how to integrate all different elements. One thing I know is that it is right timing. During the integration process, the important thing is to develop deeper meaning myself. Jeff does not just give any meaning to me, instead he implies that I will have my own meaning and it will come to me. He trusts my unconscious will find the meaning for me. Based on his trust, I have more trust in myself and I know the meaning will come from my unconscious mind. I realize that I spend most of my session focusing on my unconscious mind and body movements. At the end of this paragraph, he talks about a Western metaphor. He brings the cultural difference back into our conversation. For me, it is a signifying moment when he talks about the gut feeling. In the previous section, I said that something strong comes from the bottom of my body, and Jeff turns this into a Western metaphor. The use of this metaphor fosters an integration of my own Eastern culture and Western perspective. A simple yet power-ful metaphor to create something new within me. In my past experience, when any kind of integration occurs, something new, the third, becomes possible. At this moment, I am excited and waiting for something new to occur. Jeff's metaphor signifies an expectation for my deeper meaning and new discovery.

J: And once you explore that, take the telescope and go back to the path, to the mountain, to the mayflower, to the purple, and see how it transforms (*my hands slowly move from my heart down to my abdomen*), and how you can be more open in a new way, and although there's a steadiness to your head movement, as if you are really envisioning into the adventure, and Wei-Kai, what's happening now?

W: There was a painting, you are the golden mountain, the may-flower, and it's a beautiful painting, and it changes, switches to a quiet silent night. Dark, but with all stars in the sky.

Once again, I do not know how Jeff discovers my changing theme and new image. He quickly finds out something is different with my image. He does not miss a beat, and everything he says is crystal clear to my heart. Jeff offers a very important word, "transform." And I know "trans-form" is a key concept of alchemy and archetype. When Jeff says trans-form, immediately I can see a painting. Inside the painting, is a golden mountain and new things appear. It reminds me of what my Jungian analyst once told me: "When you are holding the opposite sides, patient-ly wait, the new third thing will appear." Thinking of this, I have a whole new perspective about my inner image. I am excited about my discovery, and I know that Jeff is aware of my finding.

J: Really clear and crisp stars. Universe filled with stars, a sky filled with stars.

W: And I feel gentle, feel soft.

J: You're at peace with yourself. Now power that emotion, at peace with yourself, can't possibly be described in words, can be realized in emotion.

W: (*My hands open up space.*) I feel blessed.

J: You are blessed. And you're a blessing.

In a moment like this, I do feel like I am blessed. I can enjoy this part of the journey forever. Usually I prefer to enjoy this kind of blissful moment myself, and do not want anyone to disturb me. When Jeff maintains a conversation with me, I feel like sharing my happiness, joy, and peace with a very special friend. When he says, "You are blessed, and you're a blessing," I am so touched, I feel as though I want to cry. Jeff is my mentor, my master, and he is so kind to give me his blessing, and it definitely is a great honor to receive his blessing. First, I feel gentle and soft. Then I feel very honored and happy to receive his blessing. We just exchange a few words, and my feelings go through some major shift. This blessing conversation is wonderful and powerful, and it creates a great energy to shake my whole being.

J: And how you continue to be blessing could be what's really essential and meaningful. And what's happening now?

W: I am grateful.

J: Back to where you started. Feeling gratitude. Sensing gratitude. Experiencing gratitude is really a blessing. Living a gratitude. Living grateful. Exploring adventure. And allowing that to land, allow that to come to rest. Fantastic. Take time with that. Feel that. Appreciate that. Wisdom with your hands, intuitive wisdom with your hands, your arms. Feeling your hands content, with your arms. And then realizing it is time to begin to reorient yourself, bring yourself back, and bring yourself back fully and easily, easily and completely (*speaking fast now*), reorient, take one or two or three easy breaths, and bring back some of that experience with you.

Jeff closes another loop. First, the inner loop closes, and second, the outer loop closes, and it becomes a perfect double circle. We had a wonderful journey together, and he still remembers what I said in the very beginning (I feel gratitude). He uses this word, "gratitude," as a way to bring me back. As usual, he uses a light tone, high tempo, and joyful voice to bring me out of trance. I can sense happiness and joy when he speaks. I enjoy reorienting myself as he suggests. Both of us know that we found some interesting treasure on this journey, and I am satisfied.

J: And then, Wei-Kai, here is an interesting experiment. As you open your eyes, just turn to the bookshelf and tell me the first title you see. Allow your mind to guide you, and what is the first title you see?

Just when I think the session is over, Jeff gives me an interesting task. He trusts his gut feeling, and he invites me to play this game with him. When he suggests this, I am in shock and start worrying a little bit. I know there are a lot of psychotherapy books on the bookshelf. I know these psychotherapy books usually come with titles including depression, anxiety, bipolar, disorder, etc. How can Jeff know that I will pick a good book title? He trusts his unconscious mind, he trusts me, I trust him, and I trust my unconscious mind. I know that unless I bring my wonderful experience back to reality, the trance journey may be just a good dream. When a trance can be tested and utilized in reality, then I know it works. I like Jeff's idea, and tell myself "Why not?" We both are curious what my unconscious mind will pick. Wait and see.

W: Poison medicine. (*Inside my head, I am yelling, "What? Poison?"*)

J: Say it again.

W: *Poetic Medicine. (We are both laughing.)*

J: Perfectly attuned, I would say that if you are thinking about that technique, and you are trying to put it into hypnotic language, I would say ratification. Whatever title you were going to find was going to ratify your experience.

Not only is Jeff speaking to me about ratification, he is teaching others about this technique. He turns a good session into a teaching lesson, so everyone can benefit from it. This is a good parallel technique. He says it to me, and teaches everyone else at the same time. I am very happy that my unconscious mind picks a perfect book title for my session. The whole process is surely a poetic medicine for myself. Jeff's poetic language, the painted image I created, my graceful body movements, Jeff's keen attunement, and our inspiring conversation on multiple levels, together constitute a great, beautiful session—more accurately, a poetic trance journey.

When Jeff starts talking about ratification, it serves two purposes for me. First, my conscious mind starts functioning and working again, and I can further reorient back to reality. Second, there is no better way to learn a specific technique than through one's own experience. When he says ratification, I feel like that is right, now I know how to apply this to myself, and how to increase the depth of trance. There is a Chinese saying about painting a dragon. The saying goes: "Only when you paint the eyes of a dragon, will this dragon come alive." Jeff painted the eyes of my dragon with the ratification experiment. The book title, Poetic Medicine, *really shines light into my heart and the session is lifted and promoted to a whole new level.*

W: Yes. Thank you.

J: Perfect, thank you. Question or thought?

W: Actually this time when you told me to wake up, a nice image just showed up. It's a bunch of trees, actually it's a bunch of golden fruit trees, it's shiny, sparkling, it is a forest, it is kind of connected to what you did to me last January. You guided me into the forest with the fire and the light. This time I just saw all trees and lights. So pretty.

J: A strong image is a good image. And overall what's your sense of where we started and where we come to?

When Jeff talks about the ratification technique, when "poetic medicine" appears in my eyes and my ears, I am blessed with this beautiful image.

I am immersed in a very beautiful image that I must share with Jeff. Jeff then turns this image into a Zen moment. The Zen master does not need to say a lot, one question at the right time is more than enough. That is what Jeff does to me. Just when I think it is about time to have a real ending, Jeff throws me a most important question. I know that before the trance really ends, it is a perfect time to tell a story or deepen some experience. I just do not know anyone who can do more artful work than Jeff.

His question—where we started and where we come to—creates a nice confusion and a light trance feeling within me. I find that it is interesting to push myself to go even further when I think this is the end. He says, "Overall what's your sense of where we started and where we come to?" This is an excellent Zen question, and at this moment I have no idea where I start from and where I am going. I don't know the answer, and I have no desire to find the answer. I know that I don't know, and I am perfectly fine with the "I don't know" state. I enjoy being unknown at this particular moment. Answering Jeff's question is very simple, I just present myself, I am here and now. Yet, to take the image to the level of verbal expression is not so easy.

W: We started with nothing and we came back to nothing. Along the journey, there are so many things happening. I settle in. I don't know where in my body it feels. It's here (*the stomach*). I got what I want.

J: How do you say in Mandarin "nothing?"

W: Kong, Kong Wu (*nothing, emptiness*).

Jeff uses a Western metaphor in the middle of session, and now he switches to an Eastern concept to give the session the icing on the cake. In Chinese Taoism, emptiness means everything is possible. It is nothingness, and yet it includes everything. It holds both ends simultaneously. When it is a Zen moment, language is not necessary—simply being is good enough. Both Jeff and I know something cannot be said or be told. Things that can be said are not true, things that are true cannot be said. Once you say it, then it is not true anymore. My experience is true, genuine, and authentic. I am very grateful that Jeff understands and that he is here to witness everything and to signify multiple meanings. It is a moment for the two of us just being, being here and now, enjoying connection, simplicity, and openness.

J: Very important in the Tao. Kong.

W: Yeah.

J: Kong Wu (*with hand gestures*).

Comment

When Jeff conducts the trance induction during this session, he does not use long sentences. I think the reason is, in part, because I am native Chinese speaker, and English is my second language. He is very thoughtful about language and cultural barriers. He somehow turns/transforms this language barrier to the advantage of hypnotic induction. His induction is precise, magical, wise, and powerful. The way he speaks is musical, soothing, aesthetic, and poetic. He does not give me a "wise talk" or teach me about life, instead he inspires me to find my own truth, my own meanings, and my own wisdom. His wording is just like Chinese acupuncture, right on the point, and it goes deep to signify all emotions and archetype energy. In Chinese, we say that Chi starts flowing after good acupuncture. What Jeff's leading and questions do for me serves the same function as Chinese acupuncture. I feel my Chi start flowing and creative energy starts flowing as well.

The ending of this session is very interesting to me. Every time I feel it is about to end, Jeff finds a way to further signify meanings and images. When I expect the ending is near, he says something and creates another deeper experience. The feeling of an endless loop is just like life itself. Life always brings me something new, something interesting, and it is a generative process. Jeff uses this session to show me that I can be generative and creative. Whenever I think it is the bottom, I can always go deeper and further. I can sense that his tenderness, playfulness, and fierceness are all on the palette, and I am free to choose and create my own painting.

Two years later, when I review this session, I still find Jeff's wording so simple and easy to understand. Every word is a drop of water slipping down to the pond and creating ripple after ripple in my unconscious ocean. Two years later in the New York City Master Class, I have another session with Jeff, and I find that there is so much more inside for me to discover. In this 2017 session, Jeff echoes with my trance and says, "I am I." Jeff and I both hit a jackpot, and we both sing, "I am I." In Chinese, "love" is pronounced as the English word "I". So I am chanting, "I am love," as he is singing "I am I." Once again, the collective unconscious goes through us and creates a meeting between East and West. That is another interesting story for another time.

Tobi B. Goldfus

Maybe it is because I first became aware of Jeff Zeig at the very first Evolution of Psychotherapy Conference in Phoenix, Arizona in 1986. He was the young compelling architect of that memorable gathering, which hosted many of the masters in the psychotherapy field from all over the world, and was known later as the Woodstock for Therapists. I, young and seeking my own psychotherapy career, got on a plane (I could barely afford the ticket). However, in return I was able to sample, listen deeply, and take in an unforgettable array of keynotes and workshops by diverse and wise sages, some now gone, and all legends in the field—Minuchin, Masterson, Haley, and Satir, to name a few. I also got to hear fascinating tales of this man of wonder, Milton H. Erickson. His brilliance, power, and magic in hypnotic experiential work had so profoundly affected and confounded those who knew him, and they wanted to understand more as they were coming into their own. And Jeff Zeig was singular in his dedication to the legacy of his mentor.

Yes, I had read Haley's *Uncommon Therapy* and had learned NLP in postgraduate trainings. Yes, I was learning CBT, was in psychoanalytic supervision with another innovative master, Herald Searles, MD. But the Ericksonian "Ranch" of orientation let me utilize all I knew, didn't know, and was going to know as I went along. I entered the Ericksonian orbit, immediately realizing that I had found the space to grow in my professional work and personal life. It was like coming home.

Then, too, there was raising my son and maintaining a full-time practice, which meant studying Ericksonian hypnosis whenever I could, in whatever format. I was fortunate to experience my first real hypnosis training with the esteemed Michael Yapko, which lasted several years. I also found time to attend numerous brief therapy conferences and workshops facilitated by Jeff, as well as stress reduction and mind/body mindfulness training at the Harvard Mind/Body Institute.

It wasn't until the Evolution of Psychotherapy Conference 15 ago, however, that a handmade flyer for a Master Class in NYC appeared, half-hidden under some other promotion. This humble flyer caught my eye like a neon light. Would I ever be accepted to something called a "master class," I asked myself. Of course, I knew full well that as soon as I got home I was going to call the contact number for a Helen Adrienne. Possibility and an exciting unknown pulled me hypnotically in.

When I called Helen and talked with her about my background I was surprised to hear her say I was more than qualified to attend the NYC Master Class. I got on a train to NYC, feeling inhibited yet curious.

I walked down the hall of Helen's apartment building on that first morning. The door knocker seemed to loom very large at the end. What will be behind that door? I took a deep breath, hesitated, and knocked quietly. As the door opened, Helen greeted me warmly, her sunshine spilling out into the hallway, as she drew me inside.

I sat listening, observing, and obsessing about how I would have nothing to say, nothing to offer, nothing to share, when I began to notice that this group of 12 (plus Jeff) were something beyond themselves. Each one seemed to have a presence that was enriched by, made more, by the group.

And, over time, this sense was born out. Every session was like a collage, a furious warm container in which we grew in each other's company, right then and there. We could, if we chose, make the experience a deeply personal uploading for change.

That first weekend, I decided to jump in, "forget about it." When I worked with Helen as her therapist (her extraordinary generosity to newcomers was apparent then and has never wavered), the room went away and I became "experiential," as I totally forgot about the audience.

Because seeing the "master" in all of us, no matter how experienced or inexperienced, is how Jeff Zeig has nurtured, honored, challenged, broke rigidities, seeded and lit the underdeveloped parts, pushed the hesitating, fired up our potentials and created a living vortex that has swept each of us up wherever we are on our professional and personal journeys, and the absolute experience of this, when it happens, is nothing short of evolution.

The trivial and mundane sit next to the profound. Confusion before clarity. Hesitation before beaming from the mountaintops. Doubt loses to empowerment. Anger, fear, shouting from the inside out, laughing, singing, dancing, being irrelevant, emoting, experiencing deep pain, and the spirit of trance transforms us, even when we aren't feeling it—and crazy lots when we do.

Sometimes Jeff is tired. Sometimes we are all tired. Sometimes we are drifting off, even napping. Maybe we are crunching, accessing back channels, checking our phones. But we are always being pulled back in, we "hear and absorb," no matter how conscious, distracted, or resistant we may be. Early on in my pilgrimage to this class, I was sitting on a bench next to Jeff, and all of a sudden, his dead weight shifted onto me. I realized he had fallen asleep, it was toward the end of an intense day. I nudged him a few times, he alerted, and immediately absorbed into the right moment at the right time. For some reason, I felt more connected to Jeff, less intimidated. Over the years, he has encouraged, nudged, and pushed me. I have expanded my self view, my confidence, come more into my potential, my vision open-ended and evolving. I have left, for the most part, "the Menno in me that represented my self-effacing and equivocating parts." After a few years of whining about not getting my book written, Jeff looked at me with a raised eyebrow, "Just write the 'f——ing' book, Tobi." I wrote it the next year. Jeff has become a mentor, a consultant, a friend.

This is not easy stuff for him. Being "on" and so focused, Jeff elicits strategic change so profoundly with whomever he is tuned into, and let us not forget, it is hard hard fricking work! This is four days of twelve of us in four roles (once as his patient, each of us being a therapist to one in the class, once being a patient with a peer therapist, once as a supervisor to a peer therapist).

During Master Class, we are in a moving, fluctuating, trusting and shifting lens, magnetized and pulled in. When we leave, no matter how profound or perhaps even uneventful a day may seem, something has happened, something has been touched, experientially and post-hypnotically.

It took me a few Master Classes to let myself go when Jeff worked with me. I was unable to relax and let the theme take me where it led. But once I could, he got me. He knows I do better work inside when I move on the outside, it is the artistic space I can delve deep into. I can't believe the stuff that has come out of me, my mouth, my actions, my deliveries, and yes, my ability to take in deeply and in life-changing ways.

We become BFFs within that space for that time, sharing intimacies, bubbling up with vulnerabilities, letting it rip. We sing to each other, take our "footprints," laugh, give support, hold each other up. We are a family when we are there, but one that is working it out, not bickering, helping to help launch each other toward a life improved, a life "changed."

We have history together, we have become a frame of reference for each other. We have grown, we have evolved, and Jeff has too. We have been through children leaving home, aging, the grief of losing loved ones, marriages, marathons, divorces, you name it. We have written books, become presenters, done our work better, let go, and enjoyed living freer. When we are at the same conferences, the world over, we are like the supportive peer group every child has ever dreamed of. We hang out, come to each other's workshops, have dinner together—we are there for each other. We keep each other's secrets.

Some great friendships have developed from first sharing our intimacies, "the good, the bad, and the ugly," being accepted and giving it back (both in ourselves and with the others) in Jeff's NYC Master Class.

As hard as it is to describe on paper, Jeff's extraordinary gen-

erosity, brilliance, and strategic and experiential artistry have giv-
en all of us the gift of becoming and evolving to our highest power
as we continue our sojourn. Erickson's dedication to encouraging
positive personal and professional development lives strong with
Jeff's own voice and wisdom. How lucky are we to have been in this
NYC Master Class universe. Beyond words, infinitely. More, it is so
that this universe now lives inside me, continually fostering my own
evolution revolution.

CHAPTER SEVEN

On Preparing for Heart Surgery

Christoph Sollmann

When Jeffrey K. Zeig first worked with Martina (an attendee of the Master Class), she was about two months away from major heart surgery and was understandably worried about the surgery itself and its outcome. When Jeff asked her about her expectations she expressed concerns about the possibility that the surgery could fail and the different ways in which it could go wrong. Jeff listened carefully to her anxieties and explanations.

At that time, I was a novice in practicing Ericksonian Hypnosis and therefore I paid attention to the process and asked myself how Jeff would guide Martina toward new perspectives on the surgery. In general I wanted to know how he would put Ericksonian Hypnosis into practice. Milton H. Erickson is closely associated with the utilization approach. Utilization is the core concept of Ericksonian Hypnosis. In particular I wanted to know if Jeff's practice would be more strategic or intuitive. Crucial to me was how he would realize multi-level-communication (Yapko, 2003). By this I mean how he would make direct and indirect suggestions and ultimately how he would realize conscious and unconscious communication during the session.

I have to admit that my view on the process and the categories I use in my observation are subjective. And, of course, I do not know if any other attendee would have a different opinion on this session. Further, I could not be sure whether Jeff himself would entirely agree with my categorization. Moreover I wasn't really sure whether this session would answer all my questions. I guess at that time I had a lot more questions than this. This was the first time I had joined Master Class so I wanted to learn as much as possible. The citations in this text are taken from notes provided by another attendee, Dana Lebo. She took copious notes throughout the four days of the workshop, a tremendous feat, for which she deserves sincere gratitude. I have abbreviated the notes occasionally for accessibility but I have endeavored to convey the genuine meaning of every single citation. This report is an excerpt from a session that took place in New York in July 2008.

After Jeff had listened to Martina's concerns and her reflections on the special intervention the surgeons planned, Martina explained that a valve in her heart needed to be reconstructed because it no longer closed properly. She described that it had affected her physical strength and performance over the last months, resulting in a gradual decline that eventually necessitated surgery to halt further decline. Martina also mentioned her other fears—of post-operative pain, of what might happen during anesthesia, and of the complete loss of control during the operation.

The Interaction

Jeff starts his intervention with a reframing, encouraging Martina to leave a negative scenario that had frightened her and enabling her to become reoriented to focusing on her resources and strengths.

Jeff: So when we're here, you can think of what can be, and we can find out there are a good many of people who've had the procedure.

He invites Martina to switch from the individual focus on her pre-surgery trepidation toward an empiric view that considers all the patients who have benefited from this kind of operation without any adverse effect. As Martina had previously mentioned the importance of her family and friends, Jeff's intervention concentrates on Martina's sociability and the positive influences of her loved ones. I notice that Martina becomes more and more aware that she could alter her perspective from that of a reflexive superficial fear to a "you-never-walk-alone-perspective."

In the next intervention, Jeff offers an indirect suggestion:

Jeff: I recommended this to other people, find people, talk to them...

Jeff additionally binds her attention through an embedded command when he states:

Jeff: Find out about what the rehabilitation will be like...

Simultaneously he highlights her education by challenging her:

Jeff: I don't know how educated you are.

Martina reacts to this remark by enumerating the resources she has access to: spiritual, symbolic, the love and support of her family, and the fact that she is well informed on the procedure (simultaneously realizing this as she explains it to Jeff)—from briefing with doctors, her research on the internet, and her confidence in the surgeon's expertise and her choice of a modern clinic that is specialized in cardiac surgery. She also emphasizes the merits of the rehabilitation clinic she planned to attend.

In trance, encouraged and challenged by Jeff's question, Martina reestablishes her locus of control, and is no longer in the thrall of her fears of the operation but is aware of her own agency and her ability to be in control. This is tremendously significant as it allows her to switch to hope and resilience.

Jeff asks her questions relating to the procedure, for instance, what will the doctor's preparation be and how will she ensure she is mentally prepared to face the surgery:

Jeff: And what are you doing to prepare?

In response Martina shows him a selection of small gems she is wearing on her necklace and a small jade Buddha that she keeps in her pocket. Then she reflects on how she has changed her behavior and attitude to life and also her attitude toward her relationship and how this has enabled her to calm down and become more mindful and "softer." Jeff encourages her reflection on her mental resources with another question:

Jeff: How do you do that?

Again, Jeff invites Martina to focus on what she can influence rather than what she can't.

I have experienced several interventions by Jeff as part of the audience, listening and watching to him, as well in the role of a "client." Two strategies become apparent to me. The first was how he slows down the communication through the intonation of his voice and other means. This has the effect of calming Martina down during the session. Her voice becomes softer, her breathing slower, and so on. From the perspective of multi-level communication, he invites Martina to slow down emotionally. Figuratively expressed, the client's panic is like a bolting horse that the therapist attempts to ease with his calm intonation and demeanor.

The second principle that continually recurred was his tendency to repeat a core idea, mostly by repeatedly asking questions, shifting from one perspective to another, circling around the same theme. This "repeating principle" is based on how the brain functions in the learning process. The repetition causes neural wiring. Psychologically it can allow clients to alter behavior and/or reactions, guiding them to new perspectives that allow them to cope with a certain stimulus or situation.

Returning to the session with Martina, Jeff continues:

Jeff: ...so this is a change you can institutionalize... I'm beginning to orient you to realize that there is a gift that you can begin to realize—even though there's the fear sensation there's a way to live—to find the gift in the situation.

Until now, Jeff has followed Martina's "concept of life," using her potential to reveal coping strategies and discover resources by herself. At this stage he takes on a more dynamic role as the facilitator to gift-wrap (a term Jeff uses often in presentations and in personal communications to describe how the therapist prepares his or her intervention) his therapeutic strategy.

He defines her inner process as something Martina has to "orient to," meaning that she will soon change from being inactive (passive, avoiding) to taking an active role in her own destiny. Jeff defines this process as a "gift" (or gift wrapping), a term that has a positive connotation, thus reframing the situation Martina is facing.

Let me add a personal remark. It is not difficult to offer a client a positive reframe, but timing and extent are crucial in order to avoid psychological resistance and allow the client to reorient to a positive new perspective. In this case, it also makes it possible for Martina to perceive the surgery as an opportunity to regain her health rather than an occasion for anxiety, where her health is endangered and in which she has only a passive role, and thus is at the mercy of her fear of the operation.

I have learned from clients in similar situations to Martina that there is a tendency to develop a fear of the fear. This has a negative impact on the client's belief in an ability to cope with the situation. Fear engenders sensations of being crippled and paralyzed, bodily and psychologically. Everyone knows that such feelings are not the ideal starting point for dealing with threatening situations. Moreover such sensations have a very negative impact on the client, because the presence of fear means that nothing helps.

Instead, Jeff reframes this fear as being part of the process that can coexist with Martina's coping behavior—a potential side-effect of the healing process—not something that she cannot control. So this reframing gives Martina a kind of anchor that conveys to her that she is in the process of realization (on the right path). Being on that path is important, rather than lying like a beetle on its back, vulnerable to an invisible enemy, such as postoperative pain.

The art of therapeutic intervention of this kind is to convey that message without saying something like, "You don't need to have fear." As Martina was going deeper and deeper into a fearful state it was becoming threatening for her. This fear was intensified by the fact that Martina, as a professional counselor, helps other people to overcome their fear. If she were told that she need not to be afraid, she would likely insist that her fear was a reality and this tension could accelerate her belief that she is trapped. Her dilemma might be stated in this way: "If I feel this fear as a therapist and can't help myself to cope with it, I am either a lousy therapist or I am really threatened by this surgery." An intervention that goes wrong at such a crucial point can anchor clients' fears and possibly cause them to lose a little of their personal and professional self-esteem.

Jeff emphasized several times the necessity of strategic orientation throughout the whole therapeutic process. I summarize the essence of his message in this way: Everything you do throughout the therapeutic process—whether conscious or unconscious—has to be evaluated in terms of strategic relevance and goal attainment. I have watched Jeff (and other teachers) for quite a long time. At the beginning of this learning process I was trying to ascertain whether a certain intervention (for example, a demonstration by a teacher) is strategic or merely a lucky strike. Now, after looking back on many years of practicing coaching and psychotherapy myself, this difference is no longer crucial to me. I have reached the conclusion that successful therapy often consists of a whole bunch of strategic, flexibly used interventions and often a good portion of luck, sometimes found by intuition and other times by chance. A therapist able to mix all these elements into something palatable and effective is doing a good job. If a therapist (or coach or counselor) is able to realize a minimum of 60 percent of mixing up the ingredients well (within the right timing and dose), he or she is a good therapist. If the degree or realization is 80 percent or even more, the therapist is excellent. The sustainability of the therapeutic relationship is a consequence of strategic interventions and outcome. In the case of Jeff and Martina, this condition is fulfilled. Jeff realized his strategic concept by gift-wrapping his therapeutic message, enabling Martina to discover the resources available to her. Jeff achieved this through consistent use of the principles I mentioned—slowing the process, repetition, and others. First and foremost, he accomplished the goal by using the utilization approach consequently.

Most therapists may know how to define the term "utilization." But what does utilization mean beyond its technical definition? Is it a method, a core concept of Ericksonian hypnosis, or an experience the therapist offers to his client? The answer to all three questions is probably, "Yes." Beyond this, utilization is the ability the therapist has to step into the client's world (or rather, to be precise, that part of his or her world which is open to the public at that very moment), finding and skillfully gift-wrapping the client's resources, even if a certain resource is lying dormant and even if it is unrecognized by the client until now. It is not rare that people ask for therapy to find resources they are not aware of. The therapist resembles the hero of the American action series *MacGyver*, famous in the 1980s and 1990s, and brought back in 2016. MacGyver is famous because of his ability to handle complex problems using simple tools, like a Swiss Army knife. The utilization approach is the equivalent of the Swiss Army knife the therapist uses to save the day, the tool that an experienced therapist can call upon in different situations to help clients find solutions within themselves.

Utilization in the case with Martina included encountering a non-native speaker with a completely different cultural background. In my review at the end of the session, I was convinced that utilization is a technique, and simultaneously a natural gift formed into an art. It is both.

In answering and evaluating my question from the start, I have to conclude that Ericksonian hypnosis as Jeff practices it is strategic and intuitive at the same time. To me both perspectives are essential to the process in general, and in particular as it was applied in the intervention with Martina.

The aspect of multi-level communication that I questioned at the beginning—how Jeff placed direct and indirect suggestions and finally how he realized conscious and subconscious communication—still has to be answered. It is written that Milton H. Erickson mastered the ability to communicate at various levels in such a way that he could simultaneously investigate conscious and subconscious intentions (Zeig, 1980; Yapko, 2003; Sollmann, 2015). In the session with Martina, Jeff realized this in numerous ways by direct and indirect means. He mentions his experiences with other people ("I recommend this to other people..."), applied an "embedded command" (Jeff probably wouldn't call it this), used variation of voice, gesture, perspective, and many other methods. How can this combination of art and science be evaluated? Could the dialogue be quantified? Could we judge it as the number of hits Jeff achieved like a boxer in a boxing match? By way of comparison, how could one assess a musician playing Bach or Beethoven? By the number of notes he or she plays or by the harmony, timing, and virtuosity? On both counts I can confirm that I learned from real Masters attending the Master Class in New York in 2008.

I have to add the ending to this particular story: Martina recovers well following surgery and she regains full health.

CHAPTER EIGHT

Of Wonder Woman and Super Grannies

Caroline Chinlund

Prologue

I searched for a session for which I had a recording and found a cd that Rob had given me. On it was written: "The keys to the castle: derive carefully."

I wondered if I had ever actually listened to it. I took my initial training in Ericksonian hypnotherapy with NYSEPH (New York Society for Ericksonian Psychotherapy and Hypnosis), graduating in 1999. Part of what I had carried with me for the intervening years was an idea that it's not important to retrieve the content of a session when trance was a major element. I usually feel that I've participated fully in all of the sessions in seminars with Jeff, whether I'm watching or actively participating. I don't usually look back, trusting that what I needed, I got.

So what an amazing experience it was to revisit this session! I am quite sure it was the one I always referred to as "the time I got reborn." Not having listened to the recording before, my memory of "reborn" was eyes closed, seeing a way of zooming back to a place, maybe even before conception. I felt in memory that I had recognized in trance that I could redo my own story and go beyond all of the places that held me in some of my limiting patterns.

Note: I've thought about how to accurately convey the feeling of the sound recording in typed form. I'm using a symbol for Jeff's "uh-huhs," which are very important in their timing, and are interspersed very often. I'm trying this rather than making a separate line for Jeff for each one. If he says more than that, I do give him a separate line. The symbol for Jeff's interjections is $(J:^{\wedge\wedge})$, and $(C:^{\wedge\wedge})$ is for mine. I use . . . . for a long pause, . . . for a medium pause, and . . for a bit shorter one. I have taken out the names of people who are in the seminar and used initials. Jeff's interjections are especially important in that they are always in the service of emphasizing or underlining the uplifting, positive parts of what I say. They are notably absent when I say something forlorn or pessimistic or blocked-sounding.

The Session

J: Where? ...In the world...

C: I could tell you a kind of, uh, ideal travel I would like to do...

J: Okay.

C: I've recently made friends with a bunch of new people $(J:^{\wedge\wedge})$, which is kind of a dream come true. $(J:^{\wedge\wedge})$ If you'd asked me—I'm not sure I've ever said it to you, but if anyone had asked me what is missing in your life, I'd have said really close female friends. $(J:^{\wedge\wedge})$. And the way I've made these friends is by being a grandmother for peace.

J: Oh yeah!

C: Yeah! So I go out into the world and get with these women and we have our mission... which is... whatever it is, sometimes it's preparing a demonstration—or sometimes it's... our favorite thing to do is called the Phonathon. And we go out into some part of the city with our cellphones $(J:^{\wedge\wedge})$, and we wear kind of Granny outfits. We look a little bit eccentric, but not so much that you'd run away from us... and we have a sort of a table with a banner around it that says, "Don't be scared... free phone calls... call your representative, tell him how you feel... troops out now... end the war,"... and we're pretty approachable, so we get quite a lot of rhythm. We meet a lot of people out on... you know, wherever we are, and it's been really hot and... it...

J: It's fun!

C: It is fun...

J: Really fun.

C: And afterwards, after we get together and... eat lunch, because we do this from 12 to 2, and then we eat lunch, and we kind of rehash who talked to whom and what they said and how we feel like more and more people are not scared to call their congressional representatives... and um... there's something about the combination of not being stuck... you know, getting into it, helping other people get into it, that has been so good for my spirits... and then, in addition, the fun, the feeding fun that we have afterwards. (J:^^). So I had this dream of travel that we would all be... um... I think of your flight imagery... that we would all be like Wonder Woman? (J:^^). You know her plane?

J: Uh huh, yup!

C: She had a transparent plane... and she could just... she had a lariat, a lasso, and she could just stand on the wing (J:^^), and she had these wonderful gold bracelets that would... I think platinum or something... that whatever she wanted to deflect (J: yep) like this, and her plane could go wherever she told it to (J:^^)... and that we would all have planes like that and we would all fly over to Iran and we would just position ourselves so nobody could touch Iran (J:^^) with any aggression while people had time to make friends y'know, and realize this is no place we want to mess up... (laughs) we've done enough messing up... so that's my dream, that's a real fantasy of friendly female power.

J: Yes.

C: That makes me feel good. When I shared it with the Grannies—I felt good!

J: Fabulous!

C: (*Pause.*) Yeah, and then the other dimension that I think I put in my goals is just that the more you are... more I, am affirmed, in that I am finding the things in my life that I need.

J: Yes.

C: And that greatly includes this new energy in my work that I've gotten through our times working all of us together (*J:*^^), the more I want to own all the goodness of that... and yeah (*J:*^^), and really let it resonate so that I can, um... be more familiar with that power, .. which is, .. I guess if I were to characterize the power of my new friends...

J: Uh huh.

C: They can carry heavy burdens (*J:*^^), they're my age or older(*J:*^^), some of them are a lot older, and they can carry heavy things for a long, long time. (*J:*^^). They can stand on their feet for hours and hours, they have this kind of endurance.

J: Uh huh.

In the following section Jeff listens and um's encouragingly as C describes a desire to open some of the spaces that are circumscribed by her WASP upbringing.

C: But I think that what I would love to incorporate...

J: Good word!

C: —is being able to take in more of the real, of the um...

J: Of the...

C: —of the real story of trauma, the real story of suffering, the real truth of what I see on the front page of *The New York Times*; sometimes it just hurts me...very much. And let the real of it come in and have its place and see where I live from there... That my nature as a WASP, brought up a WASP (*J:*^^), .. much as I really accessed my mom yesterday very much when B. was working .. and I do feel the love I have for my mother and that she had for me, but there's a kind of tamping down of the resonance that happens in WASP life… that's how we do things; the emotional resonance is quite contained, and you're not really expected to overflow very much. And I think to really take in the pain and what is real, from my people, whom I listen to, and just to hold it and see where it goes in me and them, I need all the… I need to integrate everything that I'm receiving now and say, "Yeah… this is a new place I am… I can open another door… I don't have to… I've grown! My self has changed. (*J:^^*). Yeah. It's a Granny self… (*J:^^*). I'm a grand granny self (*J:^^*) that can be ex-WASP child."

J: Yeah.

C: Now I'm… God I don't know what, but maybe… maybe… I don't know but you know my parts… you know, like my martial arts, my tai chi me (*J:^^*) that's anchoring there (*J:^^*), generating energy (*J:^^*), very thankful for having found that way of being in my body (*J:^^*), and then the playful me that really likes playing with my granny friends (*J:^^*).

C does a little more elaboration of the way the Grannies go forth as Jeff encourages.

J: Yeah… and it feels good.

C: And I know all over the country people like me are just doing this. If I think about it, what we're doing, it's happening! …and they're gonna keep on doing it… I feel it!

J: Uh-huh, fantastic! And your eyes light up when you say that.

C: Yeah… let me add one more thing! Which is that the WASP part of me wants to let go of the tamped down, encapsulated sensuality part of me (*J:^^*), the part that feels it's okay to appreciate a flower (*J:^^*), uh, but to really live in the whole realm of sexual hunger, and, um, competition, and even humor, you know, that whole space is very uh (*sighs*). . split off; it's kind of split off, still…

J: Has been.

C: Has been... (J:^^). I would like it to be invited in with every-thing else that's so good (J:^^) and uh... share it with S, my husband, and let it just generate with everything else.

Here begins the semi-formal induction.

J: Umm, so if you got the absolutely crazy idea that you wanted with malice of forethought to do a regression back to WASP central (C: Yeah), how could you do it?

C: Oh, gosh, my first muscular thought I have is compression of some kind...

J: Yeah, so you could compress yourself...

C: I could compress myself, I can unlearn how to breathe deeply.

J: You could forget your tai chi.

C: I could forget my tai chi.

J: You could forget Grannies for Peace.

You could forget your sensuality.

You could forget, you could forget, you could forget!

C: I could go, if it were safe... and why not?... I would go zooming way, way way back... (J:^^) and then I would be really com-pressed because I would be very small.

J: So, uh huh... and are you doing that now? Compressing your-self?

C: Well, imagistically I am...

J: Okay and then go with that for a minute and see where it takes you to compress yourself imagistically.

C: It's kind of taking me back to a point, you know, a point (J:^^) in space.

J: Yeah, uh-huh... and when you get to the point, in space, then what would you... discover?

C: In time. . . . I don't know maybe it's a little too abstract, but . . . . something feels very alive. I'm supposed to be going back to my WASP self (*laughs*). (*J:^^*). Being new is very lively. I'm going back and I'm alive, and... I have. . all this potential.

J: And how do you experience compressing to that WASP self? Is it something that you're seeing, remembering, feeling?

C: Really, I'm sensing myself in a kind of... it's embodied in that it starts about here. . yet it's disembodied in the way I feel that it's quite floating, quite spacey.

J: Filled with potential energy.

C: Uh-huh, a point.

J: A what?

C: A point, a point of origin (*J: Okay*) or expansion (*J: Okay*). It's hard not to take a deep breath.

J: Mm-hmm… As you take a deep breath, as you smile, what happens?

C: I want to stay with this because I think I don't have to be embarrassed about it. . . .

J: That would be a choice. . . .

C: It's as though I'm at a place before everything happened.

J: Right, and so then you can go back into that compression and experience the potential energy of it, and what happens emotionally as you do that?

C: It feels very tender.

J: Okay.

C: Very. . . . I don't know what the emotion is for feeling, "It's quite a privilege to be in this place."

J: Okay . . . .

C: It's a good place… it's saying that everything is potentially there.

J: Okay then, move forward into this granny manifestation.

C: You mean the supergranny on the—?

J: Yes with golden bracelets, the transparent plane, and the lariat, which as I remember was a golden lariat.

C: I believe so… (*J:^^*). Well, yeah, so she can't be too busy for sensuality. I guess she has to make some stops along the way.

J: Okay.

C: I don't know, maybe I could get into Iranian men, we could, all of us Grannies could (*J:^^*) appreciate the Iranian men…

J: Okay, and as you look back and get to the point of origin and as you begin to move forward and jump forward into the evolution… you see the stages of transformation of C.

C: Yeah, well there's always been a hypothesis I had… It's not that I've ever really seen it… (*J:^^*) it's just a hypothesis. It has to do with why I felt so undeserving, from such an early age. If I ever asked for anything, I needed to apologize… and the hypothesis is, and I think asking for anything is really a lot about sex, and the hypothesis was that it had something to do… really with very early needs… like maybe feeding, just that… it wasn't okay to be hungry… 'cause I was born in 1940, apparently that was kind of the style then, to not necessarily feed people when they were crying. But I don't know, if that's really what it was… but I needed food, let's say, and now to be whole—I'm pretty good the way I am, but to be whole, I would like my whole repertoire of heart-fun-genital self back.

J: Uh-huh, unapologetically!

C: Oh, yes, yeah! Unapologetically! And I feel that if I had that, thinking of D. yesterday (*session of co-participant*), if I had that it would spill over into the way my husband receives me and it would really generate some fun (*J:^^*), and some refreshment (*J:^^*).

J: So as you can reclaim that birthright (*C:^^*), and you can begin to envision how that will continue to propel your evolution in ways . . that are just fun… and I don't know exactly how you may choose to do that. . for example one possibility would be to imagine Wonder Woman, and have her go back to the point of origin... with her golden lasso, and . . . .

C: I was seeing that. I was seeing if I could do that because something about that point is made of the same stuff as the invisible plane. (J:^^).

J: So what are you doing right now?

C: Mmm. I'm seeing the plane as part of the stuff.

J: And where are you in relationship to the plane?

C: Well, I see Wonder Woman, not sure I can see me... Wonder Woman I think I have to get right...

J: So you can see Wonder Woman and she's in the plane, and which way is the plane going?

C: The plane is expanding because it's coming from the point, and the Wonder Woman is almost being born into the plane.

J: Okay and you can watch and see how the plane can emerge out of the stuff that's there at the point of origin. And how Wonder Woman herself begins to expand, along with the plane.

C: I'm seeing how much I've received from my granddaughter, who's 2½ now.

J: Uh-huh... So you can lean forward, watch, see as she progresses.... into the present time and how she lassos some experiences... like the experience of being with your granddaughter and how she can incorporate that into the stuff... (C:^^) ...transports her into a more sensuous reality.

C: Yeah.

J: And C, for a moment here's something that you might enjoy playing with... for a moment I'd invite you to be the lasso, and to go back to the point of origin and just to be the lasso or be the golden bracelets and move forward and experience yourself evolving from the point of origin, being the lasso...

C: Uh-huh... Feeling kind of like a hula hoop!

J: Okay, what is it like to be that hula hoop?

C: Well, there's a lot of necessity for lovely fluidity in the spine.

J: I'm fluid…

C: Fluid…

J: I'm spine…

C: Spine…

J: And I'm a hoop, a musical hoop at that, a hula hoop, and there's the way in which as a hula hoop you could corral things and move in that sensuous way and that you come from the point of origin, and from the point of origin you're made of the same stuff as the point of origin and you evolve… and, and if you evolve into this golden lasso that's like a hula hoop that can corral experiences, and bring them closer rhythmically and move them away rhythmically, just like a hula hoop… What's your experience now being the golden lasso?

C: I feel in focus, and in the center, of the process. . things were occurring to me that have, as I prepared to come here. . for this time. . what you call growth images, things I know that are shifting and changing and that feel very, very good.

J: Things that are shifting and really changing and that feel good.

C: Really changing, really good.

J: A really good feel, those good feelings. And then I'd like to invite you to go back for a moment to the point of origin and be the transparent plane, and to experience yourself as the transparent plane growing out of the stuff that came from the point of origin, and expanding and being a container for Wonder Woman and a transporting device for Wonder Woman… to be able to journey and develop herself from the point of origin… And what's happening now as you're the transparent plane, I'm the transparent plane and the vehicle—

C: The vehicle, and I can grow… I can shrink…

J: I grow.

C: But if I grow and I am the transparent plane, then I can feel my love for the whole earth.

J: Uh-huh…you experience a new perspective and depth of love.

C: Yeah.

J: And that some of this substance from the point of origin is some depth. . and breadth. . of love…

C: Yeah…

J: Nice to take some time, to really savor that experience, and really grasp it… the essential stuff that it is… just to be, the plane… to feel some of the growth… to experience the current of the air, the movement, to feel the Wonder Woman inside you… and to experience her as she moves from place to place, and peace to peace. . . . . What's happening now as you're the transparent plane?. . . .

C: Well, I get a little distracted by "peace to peace?" Because sometimes I guess it makes sense to land on peace for a minute.

J: Yeah.

C: Because peace is a piece. And it's shalom.

J: Uh-huh… big shalom. . . .

C: Big shalom.

J: Uh-huh . . and pax.

C: Uh-huh and pax and pox.

J: Uh-huh . . What's it like to land on peace and be there for a while?

C: Well, I feel very rich… (J:^^). A lot of good stuff is happening in my head right now.

J: Really good stuff… (C:^^). Nice to really feel that good stuff happening in your head… right now.

C: Yeah, right now. . . . I could write now… would be about… but it doesn't matter, but I could, right now.

J: Mm-hmm… You could also take some time and experience the

next landing place for the transparent plane, take it to its next destination, enjoy the journey and experience the things that you can along the path as you take the journey. . . . Do that because there's no reason in the world to do anything other than be there and in ways that are absolutely unapologetic. . . . And what's happening now?

C: Ah, well, this plane is very um... very flexible.

J: Really, really flexible.

C: Very, really flexible, so in this plane right now, I'm visiting different laps and the wish to be in laps—

J: Laps!

C: Laps, like the lap of my grandfather, and the lap of you, the lap of my analyst... that I always wanted to be in but never got to be, which is fine...

J: That's fantastic!

C: But I think it's the kind of place... you could put your granddaughter very easily, you know, in your lap... but from your lap, Jeff, I would put my arms around you and I'd be little, I'd be a little, formative creature and I would be so glad that you were here and that you could share yourself with me and with all of us and you would feel it.

J: And recycle it back to you.

C: Yeah, and it would be fun for you and fun for me.

J: Very fun to just lap it up!

C: Yeah... my grandfather in his own very WASPy way did appreciate my efforts at being a knockout female. (J:^^). It was very sweet.

J: Mm-hmm. Fantastic!

C: He nurtured those efforts, actually.

J: Okay, take it one more turn and go back and go back to the point of origin and be Wonder Woman, and really feel how you also evolve out of the stuff, and with the plane, moving forward, claiming your lasso, and your bracelets and the transportation, of the transparent plane. . . . stopping for a moment... in a place...

C:...What do you think she did for grounding? Seems like she needs some grounding.

J: Okay.

C: Always flying!

At this point Jeff seems to sense that C is losing the connection with the metaphor, and he makes a suggestion that deepens the trance experience and helps C embody it even more deeply.

J: You can see that from one perspective, but for a moment, just be her and see how it feels like from the inside... whether it feels from the inside that grounding is something that's valuable and important, and, if so, then make it so. . . .

C: Well, her feet are on the ground, on the floor, and the... plane is happening at the same time.

J: Uh-huh... And how do you sense yourself as Wonder Woman?

C: Well, I think it's in the heart . . and that's so new that the rest of me has kind of gone chilly... but I think that's where it is. That's it!

J: So you're getting it. What's it like? Going into that heart space?

C: . . . . Well, it's... pretty new... so no wonder I feel a little disoriented. It is pretty new.

J: It is pretty... and it's new.

C: Yeah, it is pretty. I had an echocardiogram the other day... Very heroic our hearts are, so heroic! Just open and close and work all the time in this beautiful dance (J:^^) and we generate these hormones, I understand, these life-affirming hormones in our hearts (J:^^) that connect us to all that nurtures us.

J: Uh-huh. . and I would invite you to be with that heroic heart, and feel the generation of all those life-affirming hormones. . and see how it warms the extremities.

C: (*In a whisper:*) Yeah! . . . .

J: What's happening now?

C: Just feels that if I. . . image being held . . and in a sense my heart is being held by me—

J: Uh-huh, I'm holding my heart.

C: I'm holding my heart. I'm surrounding my heart with protection.

J: I'm protecting my heart. I'm a container that transports and moves my heart.

C: Inspiring my heart. . (*J:^^*) . . carrying my heart around.

J: Transporting your heart and feeling the way in which your heart can continue to send those life-affirming hormones into your body and the extremities.

C: Mm-hmm . . . .

J: And then I would invite you to go back one more time and to capture the totality of the movement from the point of origin of the lasso, and the movement, from the point of the origin of the transparent plane, and the movement from the point of origin of Wonder Woman, getting to the heart of the matter and as you bring those together almost as if you were cooking, taking some of the ingredients and knowing that the ingredients as they mix together will be more than the sum of their parts . . . .

C: True . . . .

J: What do you capture?

C: Well, all of us here are much more than the sum of our parts.

J: That's right.

C: We're kind of our own organ.

J: Mm-hmm . . . . and how you can get to the essence and the real sense of the more than the sum of the parts, both personally and socially, and how you can connect with that, and how that becomes part of the mix of moving and reclaiming from the point of origin... The sensuous nature, the lariat could be a hula hoop, the transportation from the Heart of Wonder Woman... And the way that you can begin to pleasantly realize for real and for the moment, how your feet are still on the floor, your hands are resting, and you can still, still inside for the moment you feel yourself in many different ways, the warmth of the moment, and how you can experience that in your head, in your heart, in your body. And how the warmth of the moment for a little girl is different now from the warmth of the moment of a mature woman... The way in which you can memorize right now the way in which the warmth of the movement matures inside you. . . . What's happening now, C?

C: I am feeling it.

J: Fantastic, and the way you can really be with it.

C: The eyes are a very important place, too.

J: Eyes are really important.

C: Yeah, the eyes . . mm-hmm... It's okay for the eyes to radiate the warmth of the moment.

J: It is really okay ($C:$^^) for your eyes to radiate, the warmth of the moment, and you can begin to imagine yourself doing that with your granny friends, and experience yourself doing that with your husband, and your grandchildren . . . . And how it's a real luxury, and how in the lap of luxury you can take your husband, your granny friends, your grandchildren, into your lap and have them experience the warmth of the moment through your eyes.

C: Yup.

J: Why was it that you opened your eyes just then?

C: I felt full, complete...

J: Uh huh. . Huh?

C: Think so, yeah...

J: It wasn't a thought but your eyes popped open.

C: When you said "lap," I don't have the words exactly, but the feeling was feeling it's okay to be—

J: Present.

C: —present in my eyes and in me (*J:^^*). The feeling of holding you in my lap (*J:^^*) allows me to really radiate the warmth of the moment.

J: I got it! (*Laughs.*)

C: Wonderful! Thank you!

J: Pleasure.

Afterthoughts

Now that I have typed every word and observed each pause, I am in awe of the work we did that day. I think it is lovely. I noticed as I typed that Jeff's "ums" and "uh-huhs" were strategic in that they lifted my energy or spirit whenever I was talking about possibilities. He was silent when I brought up my limitations. When I say, "too much flying around, she needs grounding," he says, "You can see that from one perspective, but for a moment, just leave her and see how it feels like from the inside... whether it feels from the inside that grounding is valuable and important, and, if so, then make it so..." That intervention, amounting to a utilization of my having put some brakes on the speed of the shifting, led to a deeper place, where I sensed myself as heart.

Another piece of the way Jeff works in seminar, as I experience him, is that he chooses a set of parameters as a frame or challenge to himself for each four-day cycle with us. In this session I feel that his use of having me, in trance, experience myself as each part of the imagery I had captured, was probably a leitmotif of other sessions in the weekend. The repetitive return, with the deepening of the experience through alternate sensory channels is powerful. I'm guessing that he was illustrating for himself and others that such work is always a possibility.

There have been many seminars since this one, and my themes are often similar. I learned to speak with my heart through my eyes in part through my days on the street with the Grannies, but my sense of belonging with the street actions changed. I became more committed to being in my psychotherapy work more of the time. Now 74 years old, I am even more aware that the choices we make about ourselves in our time are important. At the time of this session I was a young Granny of 66!

The time I have spent hearing and transcribing Jeff's and my work is precious indeed. I am very thankful for having given myself the task.

Early Renaissance

Julie Ann Hall

I am in two parallel realities.

I am in the Master Class, sitting among my fellow therapists opposite Jeff Zeig. I am in a trance working with him.

I am about 60 years old. I have begun by wondering who I am, where I have been, and where I may be going.

In trance I realize I am sitting in the Chapel of St. Michel, the very small, hidden chapel across from Notre Dame in Paris. In the chapel, the red and blue stained glass windows reflect the sun across the white interior. This is one of my favorite places. It is uncrowded, still. I feel I am an in a completely different world. It is a Medieval world ruled by faith. Why am I here?

And then, suddenly, I am seeing the paintings of Lucas Cranach the Elder. Here is a very seductive Venus. She wears a gorgeous large red hat and nothing more. There is no more Madonna. Here is the painting of the Judgment of Paris as if in the early to mid-1500s. Paris is clad in heavy red velvet with a matching hat, huge and trimmed in fur. He looks very tired. He's looking up at three glamorous goddesses, Hera, Athena, and Aphrodite. He's to choose the most beautiful. Cupid flies overhead as the messenger of the gods leans on his staff. Aphrodite (Venus) offers him the love of the most beautiful woman in the world, Helen. He chooses her and thus begins the Trojan War. Now I am having fun.

All along, Jeff is asking me to describe what I am seeing, thinking. He is always calm, encouraging, nonjudgmental, curious. He is never afraid to let me, or any client, go wherever. He understands that they are/I am on an individual journey.

Lucas Cranach the Elder, early to mid-1500s, was a close friend of Martin Luther. Luther began the religious reformation, breaking from the Catholic Church. Unlike past belief, which held that man must go through a priest to talk with God, Luther believed that one could speak directly to God. This is the early Northern European Renaissance in art and in life. Art and religion are breaking free and beginning to thrive.

As am I. Yes. I laugh. I get it. I am older but I am in an Early Renaissance.

Jeff asks if I have found my answer. I say, Yes. But he says he isn't sure. He feels some real sadness deep within me. From across the room Jim Warnke says, "Don't touch it, Jeff. It's who she is." I sigh and bless him. And with that relief, that sigh, I see the fluctuations of life, the Tao.

Charles M. Iker

I'm a psychiatric social worker located in the Rochester, New York area. I attended two of the Master Classes in New York City with Dr. Jeff Zeig.

During my first Master Class, the format of the program was laid out for me, and I realized that I was going to have to participate as a therapist, patient, and evaluator during the course of the weekend. I began to feel out of my element. It felt as if I was surrounded by world-class therapists whose training and expertise far exceeded my own. Over the course of the first day and a half, I observed others seemingly begin to use hypnotic language almost effortlessly, and to say the least, I felt overwhelmed.

In retrospect, some years later, I realized that Dr. Zeig was aware of my anxiety and decided to bump me up the list in terms of taking my turn in the patient role. He then engaged me as the patient in a relaxed, encouraging, and carefree way in a conversation about me. For example, he asked me who I was, about my practice in the Rochester area, and what I hoped to learn. I remember consciously relaxing during this period. Following that, he had me engage in some mental imagery, imagining that I was an alternate version of myself; one in which I was the "me" with a lack of confidence and self-esteem, and the one with the anxiety. Then, I imagined the "me" that I would love to be—the one with confidence and self-esteem, free from all anxiety. Then, I was instructed to physically get up as myself and move toward becoming my ideal self but to have the "problem me" get in the way and stop my movement toward becoming my ideal self. All this was followed up by a conversation about why I would be stopping myself from developing and becoming a better, healthier version of myself.

After, Dr. Zeig began a session where he induced a trance and began to work with me in a hypnotic way. I do not remember all of what was said, but I remember him having me hallucinate the person that generated my anxiety in the first place; then, he had me hallucinate other people in my life who wanted to see me succeed. A great deal more was said and it affected me dramatically in a positive way; however, the exact specifics of what was said are not in my conscious memory.

In essence, as a function of my participation in the Master class, I learned a great deal about being a compassionate, caring, sensitive, nurturing human being in both my personal life as well as my clinical life. Dr. Zeig was creative, funny, incisive, and moved "things" around in my head such that it changed my perception of myself and improved my work as a clinician to this day.

CHAPTER NINE

Take a Line for a Walk

Father Jim Warnke

The Master Class with Jeff Zeig is an exercise, or rather a series of exercises, in experiential psychotherapy, and the study of the same. Hypnosis is one aspect and then there are approaches from virtually everywhere along the psychotherapeutic spectrum. Those of us in attendance share a singular intention, to master the craft we have been honing for many years, or many decades.

Before reading my notes, here, you might want to skip ahead and study the transcript of my session with Jeff. You might want to do this now, not because it is so profound—quite to the contrary I see it as pretty garden-variety therapy in the sense that it doesn't revolve around a life-threatening or overly dramatic issue in my life—but because it reveals the artful way that Jeff engages me in an experiential and healing process. As you study Jeff's work, here, you will discover that there is a great deal to learn and that learning will not come from a casual or even intensive reading. To truly absorb the magnificence of the work, to appreciate Jeff's mastery of language, to recognize the nuances of his craft, you will need to read it many times, write in the margins, make your own notes and perhaps even say the words out loud because doing so will bring the work to life, and make it a part of your own experiential learning.

What follows is a set of observations and insights I experienced in studying this session. Since I am writing a chapter and not a book, my comments will be brief. In their brevity, I hope to mirror the deftness with which Jeff works, giving just the right amount of information while leaving you free to follow whatever is emerging in your mind's eye; a space that allows you to see if my observations match up with your own or if they hint at things you might not have seen.

As you reflect on this session I invite you to note how much time it takes Jeff to really say anything. Even though he knows me well, he is listening intently, allowing me to tell my story in my own way and at my own pace. Note that he does try to slow me down several times. And I finally get this after the third or fourth time he says something, sharing that I am on pain medication and I may be overcompensating and therefore not responding as I normally would to Jeff's initial encouragement to slow down. Jeff's persistent invitation to shift out of my rushed speech eventually slows me down in more ways than one.

You may also notice the conversational tone of the session, which Jeff eventually makes explicit, marking it as conversational hypnosis, which it is. Jeff has worked with me for over ten years (approximately 20 sessions) during my twice-yearly attendance in the Master Class. He knows that I can go into a hypnotic trance at the drop of a hat and so he utilizes this and does not waste time on some lengthy hypnotic induction or patter. When he begins to speak to me as if I were in trance, I go into trance. This may not be so obvious on the printed page, but it is quite obvious in the recorded session. You might find it interesting to go over the transcript again and underline where you think the transitions into hypnotic communication begin and then consider why you think it. Without the recordings, it will not be possible for you to validate your choice points, of course, but just explaining your selections to yourself will be a fruitful exercise.

As the session progresses, Jeff begins to introduce threads of ideas of his own, and to pick up on threads of ideas of mine, and to note which threads I take up, and which I do not. You will discover how Jeff carefully matches stories and allusions of his daughter, when she was young, to mine of my grandson. You will also discover how he artfully collects my stories, such as the one about a particular Picasso print, so that he can utilize them as the session goes on, knowing that I will use them to make progress in what is a difficult area for me.

A few other morsels to consider: Jeff's utilization of the presence of the group to talk to me over their shoulders and to them by talking with me; and the movements among visual, kinesthetic, and auditory imagery that are intertwined during the session, as Jeff works the shuttle and peddles of the loom. I am surprised at my utilization of visual imagery at all because this is my weak link due to my visual impairment/legal blindness. Jeff's introduction of the notion of choice and decision points strikes me as important because in earlier sessions with him, especially since my retirement two years ago, I have referred to my time as more and more precious to me.

The Session

Jim: So, you look at this. This is... Can I tell you a story?

Jeff: Yes!

Jim: Okay, I will tell you the story.

Jeff: Tell me a story.

Jim: Okay, this is a true story.

Jeff: Yes.

Jim: Oops, sorry.

Jeff: Those are the best kind.

Jim: About three weeks ago, Marie and I went to a memorial service for the brother of a dear friend of ours. The brother... we knew both brothers, but...

Jeff: Un-huh.

Jim: Our friend, a little bit younger than us, has Parkinson's. His brother was like a petty bureaucrat up in the Bronx.

Jeff: Okay.

Jim: And, you know, they are an Irish couple, and so at typical Irish marrying age, Jimmy, the brother who passed away, married at age 50 a woman from Dublin...

Jeff: Un-huh.

Jim: She had a daughter, they were happy for five years, and he got pancreatic cancer and died.

Jeff: Oh boy.

Jim: The funeral was in Dublin but there was going to be a memorial mass, so Marie and I went. The mass was in the basement of the University Church at Fordham—

Jeff: Un-huh.

Jim: —where Marie goes to mass on Sundays in the upstairs church, and this was the chapel where she and I were married.

Jeff: Un-huh.

Jim: I hadn't been there in 40 years, okay... you know they re-did it a little bit, but anyway...we were there, we're early, we're in the back with relatives, and a woman comes up and she says, "Excuse me, aren't you Jim Warnke?" I say, "Yeah," and she says, "I'm Pat and I was your student at Aquinas High School here in the Bronx in 1969, and you taught the Marriage and Sex Ed program in the Religion Department—

Jeff: Un-huh.

Jim: "—and I will never forget the lesson you taught. You brought in a print of a painting by Picasso called *Picasso's Bouquet*...

Jeff: Un-huh.

Jim: "—and you told us—

One of us has pulled up a picture of the lithograph (actually titled Bouquet of Peace*) on an iPhone and I ask Jeff, "Do you want to pass that around? It is an audiovisual. That's all right."*

Jim: "—and you showed us the painting, you know, we were from the Bronx, we never saw paintings, and you explained how you had received it as a wedding gift from your wife's roommates—
Jeff: Un-huh.

Jim: "—and because you couldn't see it very well she had to describe it to you and how, you know, it was actually two people, not one person holding the bouquet, but two—"

Jeff: It could be three.

Jim: You know, right, and she said, "You know, you told us that, that a relationship was a fragile thing like a bouquet—"

Jeff: Un-huh.

Jim: "—and that to be successful both people had to have at least one hand on the relationship at all times and that in the painting you couldn't tell who was giving the flower and who was receiving it," and she says, "You said a whole bunch of other stuff but that is what I remembered," and she says, "You know after high school, I actually spent some time as a Dominican sister. I never got married, I taught in their schools and stuff, but I have done a lot of religious education. I still do and whatever I do, the thing about marriage, I always use that."

Jeff: Un-huh.

Jim: And I'm thinking, "Holy crap, that was 46 years ago." Okay. I look at Marie, she looks at me and we smile, and people come in, the priest comes in, there's the mass and I'm thinking, you know, there is a parable about Jesus carrying ten lepers, and one of them comes back because he remembers to say thank you.

Jeff: Un-huh.

Jim: Because the healing doesn't happen right away, it is on their way to the temple, and I thought, "Every once in a while God sends you one of these so you don't lose heart."

Jeff: Un-huh.

Jim: So the mass is over and we are getting ready to go into this little side room for a little food, and a guy comes up and he says to Marie, "Are you Marie and Jim Warnke?"

Jeff: Un-huh.

Jim: You know, yeah. He says, "In 1973 I was a student here and you guys came and gave a talk on a Pre-Cana marriage thing." He says, "I wasn't engaged yet, my fiancée wasn't there because she wasn't my fiancée, but I was thinking about it, and you brought this print of *Picasso's Bouquet*, and you talked about how you couldn't tell who was giving and who was receiving, and you talked about, you know, how both people had to have a hand on it," and it was like word-for-word. So, Marie and I are kind of looking at each other, and then he leaves. After repass he drags his wife over and she says, "Oh, he talked about this forever. He bought it for me as a wedding present. It has been in our bedroom ever since, and just so you know—

Jeff: Un-huh.

Jim: "—about two months ago my son said he was getting married. He was going to ask his girlfriend to marry him and we both took him by the hand spontaneously and took him in the bedroom and stood him in front of the picture and said the same stuff."

Jeff: Un-huh.

Jim: Now this print has hung over Marie's dresser in every place we have ever lived for our entire married life. So, we get in the car and of course we're looking at each other and she says, "Do you remember doing a talk in Bishops Hall?" I say, "I can't even think of who would invite us to do that. The Aquinas thing made sense," and I was pleased and she was quietly pleased although she didn't say so until later. In that second bit, she was the one who was recognized first. I was the one who was recognized second, and it was just an amazing thing. So you know how things hang in your bedroom…

Jeff: Un-huh.

Jim: You know, after a while you have a negative hallucination. You just walk by and okay...

Jeff: Un-huh.

Jim: And the following Sunday I actually dragged it into church and used it as a sermon prop—

Jeff: Super.

Jim: —because one of the themes was marriage, and relationships and all that crap, and I just... I cannot walk past it without... I mean I can't really see it, but I mean I really can no longer walk past it, and I realized, you know, the times in our life together when our relationship was at its most difficult were probably the times when I stopped seeing that, when I stopped noticing that—

Jeff: Un-huh.

Jim: —going by. Okay, so that is here. Okay. (*Here, I hold out my hand palm up as if physically holding this story.*)

Jeff: Un-huh.

Jim: Here, a 2½ year old Thomas Miguel Leahy, my new deputy assistant spiritual director... (*Here again, I hold out my hand palm up next to the first story as I begin the next, as if holding an object.*)

Jeff: Who is living with you?

Jim: Who is living with us with his mom, Judy.

Jeff: Who you adopted.

Jim: Who we have legally... yeah. We've neglected the legal part, but we're Grandma and Grandpa, and we love it, and I am learning all kinds of things with him. I am getting a second chance at all kinds of things. As you know, Grandpa, you get second chances that you didn't get the first time out.

Jeff: Un-huh.

Jim: And so, what he has been teaching me now that I need to know...

Jeff: Un-huh. Thomas.

Jim: Okay. So this Picasso and that whole experience—

Jeff: Un-huh.

Jim: —that is here, and so here is... okay... when he was a little baby he needed to be cuddled and swaddled, back when he was a little bitty baby... okay, now he is 2½...

Jeff: Un-huh.

Jim: His favorite words are, "no," "mine," and, "I did it." Okay.

Jeff: Un-huh.

Jim: And it's really interesting to watch Marie, how you can play those three things against one another...

Jeff: Un-huh.

Jim: The other Mrs. Erickson, as I think of her...

Jeff: Un-huh.

Jim: Anyway, but what I'm saying, a couple of things with Thomas, so for the snow—

Jeff: Are we in a hurry here?

Jim: Okay, I'm not.

Jeff: Okay good.

Jim: We're outside and he has a swing, okay—

Jeff: Un—huh.

Jim: —and now he is sort of experimenting with the big kid's swing as opposed to the little kid's swing. I mean he kind of lies on his belly and twirls around on a big kid's, but on either side it is like a stepladder...

Jeff: Un-huh.

Jim: So he climbs up, and he loves to climb up and down and up and down. One of the things that I admire about this child is his persistence.

Jeff: Un-huh.

Jim: He is incredibly persistent. Then there was this one day, he was climbing up and, you know, I don't hold him anymore, but I spotted him, okay, because he gets tired or, you know, it is cold or whatever.

Jeff: Still needs protection.

Jim: Still needs protection, but it is a different kind, okay, and it involves my saying, as I listen to him saying, "I can do it," saying, "Yes, you really can." Right? Then after about the 47th time this particular day, he climbs up, and I can tell he is getting tired, right, and I was about to ask him if he wanted me to take him down and he said, "Pop Pop," and I said "Yeah," and he just let go. (*Laughter.*)

Jeff: He knew you'd be there.

Jim: Yeah. It never occurred… and my experience was that it would never occur to this child, having identified my presence, that he would have to turn around and look, which was amazing, okay. So there is that and there are also the times when he gets into "no" and he is told "no" and he doesn't like it and, you know, if it is necessary we know how to cajole him and work around that stuff. But, I am also noticing that sometimes what he needs from me, not the two ladies in the house so much, is I mean, I still do the workarounds, Marie does the workarounds, his mom can do… she is learning from Marie to do the workarounds. It is not like I don't know how—

Jeff: Right.

Jim: —but I find myself going, "No, you can do that. I can wait."

Jeff: Un-huh.

Jim: I am not asking about it…

Jeff: No, you can do that.

Jim: Whatever, like, you know, his mom came down last night, he was ready for bed, and we have a cuckoo clock in the hallway and he wants to pull on the strings. Marie will let him when she is there to hold his hand, but I, my tactile is not that good anymore, so when he is with me it is, "No, you can't touch it." So he will turn away and, "Uhmmmmmmmmm," you know. He usually won't scream and cry but he is like, "Mmmmmmmmmmmm..."

Jeff: Grumpy.

Jim: And so on, and the only thing that happened is you got told no, you'll live. I say that actually. He is 2½ but I am going to say the words.

Jeff: Okay.

Jim: Now, his mother came and she was exhausted and I needed to do a workaround. My favorite workaround with this is he will sometimes lie on his back or he will just sit with his legs out, and I will grab his feet and, you know, I will tilt him back to his head and his back is on the floor and I will start to drag him across the floor and I'll go, "My life is terrible... it is just unbearable. Grandpa told me not to touch the strings, everyone hates me..."

Jeff: You're saying this?

Jim: I'm saying this.

Jeff: Yes.

Jim: "The world is evil and bad," and then I'll go, "bump bump" and I'll bump his butt on the ground, and after two bump bumps he's laughing.

Jeff: He's good.

Jim: That's a workaround.

Jeff: Yes.

Jim: But I'm waiting more and more when it doesn't involve his mother. You know, I'm not going to let him decompensate.

Jeff: Right.

Jim: But it's like, "No, you can find it within yourself, to reconstitute." Right?

Jeff: Yeah.

Jim: Right. It's just hard.

Jeff: Yes.

Jim: That's all it is. So, it is there, Picasso's Bouquet. Last bit here...

Jeff: Although with the Thomas part, Dad's poke, and Mom's stroke...

Jim: And Mom's stroke.

Jeff: And you're poking...

Jim: And I'm poking, right.

Jeff: Which is a workaround.

Jim: I can do the workaround, which is more stroke-esque... but it's the poke...

Jeff: Okay, got it.

Jim: But it's the poke, and then there's me, okay, kind of observing. Being a participant-observer, both here and here. (*Marking the two places with my hands.*)

Jeff: Yes.

Jim: And thinking to myself, "Okay, if my inner child hasn't been cuddled enough by now, I'm going to die before this kid gets out of diapers." I was listening to Sue work... I mean, I forgive me, because we are both preemies, my sense is that preemies walk around with an umbilical cord in hand—

Jeff: Un-huh.

Jim: —looking to re-attach it—

Jeff: Okay.

Jim: —and that can be life work, and it is a futile life work. It is a quest for the holy grail. There is none, you cannot crawl back in the womb, you can't. That's done.

Jeff: There's not enough belonging in the world. There's not enough attachment in the world. There's not enough stroking in the world.

Jim: Right, there isn't enough because it's not about amount, it's about specificity.

Jeff: Un-huh.

Jim: And you can get some workarounds—

Jeff: Okay.

Jim: —a little compensation here and there, all of which is good, useful and important—

Jeff: Uh-huh...

Jim: —and okay...

Jeff: Yes.

Jim: So, whenever I look at a 2½-year-old, I also see kind of like a 14-year-old...

Jeff: Okay.

Jim: You know, that mix, you know, put on your big boy pants—

Jeff: We're not in a hurry, right?

Jim: I'm not in a hurry.

Jeff: Okay.

Jim: When I look at this, I go "Oh, I can't tell who is giving, who is receiving, and it presumes equality." It presumes... you know, there can be temporary or—

Jeff: Give and take...

Jim: —situational dependence, you know. Marie is never going to agree to me driving a car, but look at the frame, there has got to be this or it whatever it is, it is not.

Jeff: With Marie?

Jim: Yeah, with Marie… and then the last bit is here, okay, and, you know. I find it remarkable and it happened around my commitment to do a chapter from the book we have been talking about and my not doing it, and I made several serious passes at it… (*Again, I hold out my hand palm up, making a line in the air of these three stories.*)

Jeff: Un-huh.

Jim: You know, that I sat down and ate worms and just decided it was more than I could manage and that was that.

Jeff: Un-huh.

Jim: Okay.

Jeff: No workaround needed.

Jim: And this was something that I want to do, so sometimes wanting to do something is enough of an incentive to get a person over that.

Jeff: Okay.

Jim: Okay. There are people in this room that when Rob makes a commitment, the sun will stop—

Jeff: Yes.

Jim: —rising before that happens.

Jeff: Yes, un-huh.

Jim: When I make a commitment, I am pretty sure that it's not going to happen. A deadline for me is just something to feel guilty about as I roll over it.

Jeff: Un-huh.

Jim: No, I'm really serious. I mean there is homework from the sixth grade that I haven't turned in yet… You know, put any human being in front of me who may be in need and I can respond to that. But take any project that I am interested in and it gets too hard really fast, okay, and I don't want to be as successful as the rest of you are.

Jeff: Un-huh.

Jim: I really don't, but I would like to finish the chapter in the book because I really would like to be part of this.

Jeff: Okay.

Jim: And I've been whining for five years about writing, and you know, this year I wrote two poems, "What a great boy am I!" I am pleased with that, and yet that seems like pitiful for a grown man and, so...

Jeff: In terms of the quantity of productivity.

Jim: Of the quantity of productivity, yes...

Jeff: You like the quality.

Jim: The quality is pretty good with the poems. I like them. I submitted them to a contest.

Jeff: Ohhh!!

Jim: I don't know whether they are going to win anything. I really don't care. You know, I was interested enough in the contest to submit them—

Jeff: Wow!

Jim: —and no more.

Jeff: Yeah.

Jim: But, I'm interested in... 10 years ago when they were still doing VHS tapes, I bought a calculus course from the teaching company... because I crawled through high school math and went to summer school for three years to get through, you know, three years of high school math and I got like the lowest grade ever recorded in calculus at Stonehill College in Massachusetts, and I decided, which for me is always a mistake, I decided that

I didn't want to die having had calculus defeat me, and I just didn't care—

Jeff: Oh yeah.

Jim: —how many times I had to go through the course, I was going to figure it out. Well, I gave those tapes away after about three tries and never getting past lecture 5, because frankly by the time I got to 5, I realized that I didn't... you know, when you go to a lawyer's office and you know that they are speaking English—

Jeff: Um-hmmmm.

Jim: —but you have no idea what they are actually saying, that was the thing and it was just enough.

Jeff: With calculus, the first time through you know that you don't understand it—

Jim: Yeah.

Jeff: —the second time through you think you understand it, and the third time through you don't understand it, but you don't care because you can still do something with it.

Jim: Okay, and for me I just repeated the first half of the first part multiple times—

Jeff: Got it.

Jim: —and yet I just gave up on it... I just... and so there is a part of me that when I see how persistent Thomas is...

Jeff: Yes...

Jim: Okay. I admire it because I am not. The closest that I seem to be able to get to persistence... now—

Jeff: NNNN... NNNNN... NNNN... install a warning indicator.

Jim: —is to not quit. Okay... is to be a minimalist and just not quit.

Jeff: Un-huh.

Jim: So, again, I know this. I am trying to figure out whether this is something that I really can work within and have some success with or I just need to decide, you know what, you're 68 and this is the way you are, calm down.

Jeff: With the chapter?

Jim: Well, with the chapter. So, I am laying this, this, and this and hoping... (*Now again gesturing the three things before and between Jeff and me.*)

Jeff: Yes.

Jim: First of all, you're the therapist, and you can do whatever the heck you want...

Jeff: Yes.

Jim: Whether it's in a trance or whether you want me to get up... by the way I'm on my second oxycodone or the medication is just... I'm not feeling well today.

Jeff: Maybe that is why you are speeding up a little bit.

Jim: Okay, is that what I am doing? I haven't noticed. Thank you. Okay. I am probably overcompensating... I need to slow down.

Jeff: Un-huh.

Jim: I can move a little, but I cannot get on the floor.

Jeff: I don't need you to move to do this.

Jim: But...

Jeff: Well, now...

Jim: Okay.

I had not understood in the moment that Jeff had allowed me to entrance myself with my own stories. I feel a shift in the session.

Jeff: What... what are you placing? I've got the quilt... I've got the pieces. I understand the pieces, and now one part of this is that you have a tremendous responsibility to me, to Sue, to Rob, etc., etc., to Helen. You have to do the chapter.

Jim: Yeah, I know. I have to do the chapter, or disappoint you all again. Those are my options.

Jeff: Well, uh-huh. Well, for one, I'm not part of the disappointment crew so I don't give a flying fuck whether or not you do the chapter.

Jim: Okay, well that's helpful.

Jeff: Un-huh. I would be glad to have your chapter, should—

Jim: Yeah.

Jeff: —you want to contribute it. So now, where could you imagine Thomas, if you are putting him as an entity inside your body, at this moment? (*Shifting from remembering to having an experience in the moment.*)

Jim: What immediately comes to mind is something that I can't actually do physically, and that is something that I loved doing with my own kids when they were little, which is having them on my shoulders.

Jeff: Great. So, imagine Thomas is on your shoulders and imagine Thomas is looking at that perspective on this idea of doing the chapter, and be Thomas for a moment and say, "Oh no...no nuh nuh no... no nuh nuh no... no nuh nuh nuh no... no nuh nuh nuh no... no NO... no nuh nuh no... no nuh nuh no... no nuh nuh nuh no... no nuh nuh nuh no... no NO..."

Jim: No, nuh, nuh, no... NO nuh nuh no... no nuh nuh nuh no... no nuh nuh nuh no... no NO... (*Spoken in toddler language.*)

Jeff: And mine... mine... mine... MINE...

Jim: Mine, mine, mine, MINE... (*Again, spoken in toddler.*)

Jeff: And keep in mind the chapter as you're doing that, and be 2½... and what happens if you do that?

Jim: I flash immediately to something that happened a couple of months ago. So we come down for breakfast in the morning, we get up with them, and Judy, she is running around, she is making breakfast for him and for her and trying to get ready to go. She has got to get him to daycare and into work. She has made him pancakes and he says, "No... no... no..." He's not rude, he's just very definite and Marie goes and gets a kid's place mat that has got the alphabet and an animal's name next to each letter, aardvark, you know, bear, right...

Jeff: Sure.

Jim: "Thomas here's some pancake." "No." "Oh, okay. The bear will probably eat it." "Mine." He ate four pancakes.

Jeff: Perfect workaround.

Jim: Yeah. Judy said to Marie, "I haven't got time now but tonight could you explain to me what just happened?"

Jeff: Yeah.

Jim: But that is what immediately leapt to mind.

Jeff: Got it. Okay, so let's... where the song came from, is Disney, "We Sing Silly Songs" and when my daughter was maybe 5 or 6, we would sing this song and it is a two-part song where the dad starts and says, "Oh yes, yes, yes, YES, yes, yes, yes, yes, yes, yes, YES, yes, yes, yes, yes, Yes, yes, yes, yes," and the girl goes, "Oh no, nuh nuh no, nuh nuh no..."

Jeff/Jim: Nuh nuh no, nuh nuh nuh no, no nuh nuh nuh no, nuh nuh nuh NO, nuh nuh nuh no, nuh nuh nuh no...

Jeff: And then eventually they switch roles, and that is the workaround.

Jim: Right.

Jeff: Un-huh... and then the little girl is going, "Oh yes, yes, yes, YES, yes, yes, yes, yes, yes, YES, yes, yes, yes, yes, Yes, yes, yes, yes." Now, when you begin to imagine what that Picasso could look like, what is in black and white is really the background, and what is in black and white is the support, and what is in black and white are the hands, and all the hands are doing in black and white is experiencing being support and the petals and the flowers, which I remember disassociated from the black and white stalks. I don't want the reality to get in the way of my delusion. (*Jeff is utilizing black and white in numerous ways; something is either/or; I see only in shadows without color; things become clearer in the space between the black and white. And I invite you the reader to notice what other ways he might be using this.*)

Jim: Oh, okay. I wanted to look at it. (*Chuckles.*)

Jeff: Yes. Uh-huh. Well, look at it in your mind and you have four flowers and I think two of them are yellow, one is blue, one is red, and that the flowers represent something about being vibrant and the choice of the colors... I'm certain that Picasso is very intentional about having two similar colored flowers, and that the moment of being an artist is to create something out of nothing that brings life, that some future entities can, in some small way, incorporate into their being. Now, it just so happens that next month... almost next month, March, I have to give a 5-minute speech at the marriage of my step-daughter, and I don't know that I will choose that particular piece of art as a metaphor to talk about but perhaps I will, and there is nothing wrong with building on one type of wizardry and making it something that can be meaningful. So, I can begin to hatch in my mind something about how to make that happen and how to make that useful and how to take something that is eminently inanimate and use art, Tezuka art, painting, or metaphoric art to make a simple idea come alive and, I suppose, that the essential phrase there is that "oh yes, yes, yes, yes, YES, yes, yes, yes, yes, yes, YES, yes" comes out of an intrinsic realization about how you want to use your art and that it would be very clumsy to do a workaround.

You could easily spend half an hour re-reading and deconstructing the above paragraph.

Jim: Un-huh.

Jeff: And it wouldn't be very interesting or effective to do a work-around, so then it comes down to choice. (*Note how Jeff shifts me away from "decision" and into "choice."*)

Jim: Un-huh, that's right.

Jeff: And should it appeal to you to spend your precious time and your precious gifts to create art out of nothing... then, and only then, can you proceed without any commitments or without any deadlines or without any structure and without any sense that you'll win the contest, and you do it just because. (*Here Jeff discards all my baggage.*)

Jim: Un-huh. I forget which conference it was. I think it was a conference in San Francisco, years ago when my son was...

Jeff: Yep, I met him.

Jim: Right. Well, this was years ago—

Jeff: Yeah.

Jim: —and I introduced him to Jeff Feldman. Jeff and I are friends.

Jeff: Okay.

Jim: And the three of us went out to dinner.

Jeff: Un-huh.

Jim: And I was very excited to have... Jeff was my first teacher at NYSEPH—

Jeff: Oh.

Jim: —and so I was very... I didn't really know him except in that context until I started meeting him when he was a presenter and I was an attendee at a number of conferences. We got to be good friends that way.

Jeff: Was this a long time ago?

Jim: Very long time ago...

Jeff: 1988?

Jim: Yeah, it could be when my son graduated from high school. My son is going to be 45 so he was... anyway, we were sitting in this lovely steak restaurant and Jeff... You know him right?

Jeff: Yes.

Jim: So, he is like a master... he is just interested in everybody. He said to my son, "So, tell me how is it that you create?" He, of course, posed questions I never asked my son...

Jeff: Right.

Jim: "Do you work from sketches, do you do this," and my son said to him, "I don't really work from sketches." He said, "There is nothing more exciting to me than standing in front of a blank canvas to see what that canvas is going to draw out of me."

Jeff: Un-huh.

Jim: He said, "I can stand there for a really long time. I can have to come back to it over days, and sooner or later I just make a mark, and then what comes grows." I was fascinated by that and today he says that he doesn't work from sketches, that's his process.

Jeff: Yes.

Jim: That is what he still does, and I remember thinking I find nothing as terrifying as looking at what would have been in those days a blank page.

Jeff: Un-huh, although that is a union of a lot of discipline that underlies—

Jim: Right... that stuff.

Jeff: —intrinsically underlies that spontaneity.

Jim: Right, and I'm not sure if the other part is true for me, but that is just—

Jeff: Right.

Jim: —what comes into my head.

Jeff: Well, you could find, if it is interesting to you, a way of referencing not only Thomas on your shoulders but… what's your son's name?

Jim: Dave.

Jeff: David—

Jim: Dave.

Jeff: David on your shoulders. (*What Jeff remembers here, consciously or unconsciously, is that my wife and I have always called our son David while he always refers to himself as Dave.*)

Jim: Yeah.

Jeff: And David on your shoulders could have an orientation that sparked you.

Jim: He took me in. Even when we visit I often sit with him in his studio, which is like half of a two-car garage, and he likes it. He says it is because he can open the door in the day time and in the night time he can close it, and he has got all kinds of incredible lighting and stuff, and he said he was doing a painting and he said he wanted me to do what he does along with his students. He said to me, "Put out some paints, take a brush, and just dip it in any paint you want, put it anywhere on the canvas," and then he said, "just take a line for a walk."

Jeff: Un-huh.

Jim: "Just see where it wants to go." But this was in a painting that he had already begun. I said, "No, no, no." He said, "You do that, and then my task becomes to find a way to incorporate that line in the larger painting."

Jeff: Un-huh.

Jim: And he said, "I like when other people do it because when I do it, it always fits." You know, and so it was amazing how much trepidation I had about just putting a line on a canvas.

Jeff: Take a line for a walk.

Jim: And take a line for a walk… it was just great, and I love the finished painting, I just really do.

Jeff: He could utilize adequately, artistically, whatever you did to take a line for a walk.

Jim: Yeah, yeah, okay.

Jeff: And if I was thinking about Wei Chi and a through-line, and a through-line can be take a line for a walk.

Jim: Okay, yes.

Jeff: Un-huh.

Jim: Okay.

Jeff: And that the permutations of take a line for a walk and the wisdom of take a line for a walk and the enthusiasm that can be generated out of take a line for a walk, building on that momentary trepidation and willing to step in to "take a line for a walk," and be delighted about how that simple act can be utilized in a very creative way, and that a simple metaphor can be a way of taking a line for a walk, and a way in which Paul Klee could take one line and create it into something, or Picasso could take one line and take it for a walk, and make it into something that was creative and artistic and that there is something that could be absolutely thrilling, something that may start as being somewhat chilling, but can be absolutely thrilling about take a line for a walk, and there is an intrinsic sense of the remarkable value of your unconscious mind in coming up with an organizing thought, an organizing principle, and that organizing principle could have relevance for relationships, take a line for a walk, and that organizing principle could have relevance for comfort—take a line for a walk. That organizing principle could have some relevance for relationships. Take a line for a walk and delight, really delight, in overcoming the immediate chill to orient to the thrill of take a line for a walk and appreciate—

Once again, take half an hour to re-read and deconstruct the above.

Jim: Un-huh.

Jeff: —the creative capacities of your inner mind to bring something that was previously inadequate to life.

Jim: Yeah, that's a really different thing. That's a really different thing.

Jeff: Mmm-hmm.

Jim: You know it's one thing to sit with somebody, even with somebody who feels pretty bad and kind of muck around until you see some little spark to blow on.

Jeff: Right, exactly right.

Jim: You know, that's—

Jeff: You do that brilliantly.

Jim: —one thing.

Jeff: Yes.

Jim: And even I know I do it well.

Jeff: Yes.

Jim: But this is like a whole other thing, I mean that oddly at this moment seems okay, but I am… am struck at the difference.

Jeff: Experiential difference.

Jim: Experiential difference… that's right.

Jeff: Yes. Which can't be really adequately described anyway, but can only be sensed, felt and realized and there is a way that you can make it yours and say, "It's mine."

Jim: Yeah. I mean, what I am doing right now is like I can get up in the morning and before I put my feet on the ground, know that I should eat like a diabetic today, and know that I am going to go off the reservation.

Jeff: Un-huh, yeah.

Jim: Another day I can get up and know that I can go to the same deli that I go to when I go off the reservation—

Jeff: Yeah.

Jim: —and be just fine.

Jeff: Yep.

Jim: And what I have been trying to track for years, but find myself doing it at this moment—

Jeff: Un-huh.

Jim: —is I know, I mean I know it, I experience the difference.

Jeff: Yes.

Jim: I can tell myself stories, I can do strategies…

Jeff: Yes, you do.

Jim: Which I do, and they work mostly with little success, sometimes, with success…

Jeff: You have to walk around…

Jim: But I'm already in this state.

Jeff: Yeah, no wall to cross. (*Here Jeff is utilizing the Christian Cross, one of the symbols of my Priesthood, with multi-layered meaning.*)

Jim: You know, so when I was young…

Jeff: Yes…

Jim: You know, and there was no such thing as videos. I could tell whether I was going to go to a porno movie tonight or whether I wasn't… I mean, I just knew when I got up.

Jeff: Yes.

Jim: And I have never found a way to shift… It seems to shift, okay, but I have not found a way to volitionally make that shift with any reliability.

Jeff: Right. There is an intrinsic sense in all of us of, "I won't if I have to, even if I want to…" (*Note here how Jeff picks up on my statement above that just wanting to do something is not enough, that wanting is not what it takes to shift states, shift experiences.*)

Jim: Un-huh.

Jeff: And it's part of our developing identity. I won't if I have to, even if I want to, and we find ways of making a shift into, "I will, because I want to," no matter who says you have to, especially if you say to yourself you have to.

Jim: Right.

Jeff: I will because I want to.

Jim: Right, okay.

Jeff: So now, no walkaround—

Jim: No.

Jeff: —is going to get you from point A, "I won't if I have to"—

Jim: Right.

Jeff: —to point B, "I will when I want to."

Jim: Right, because I don't often seem to even when I know I want to.

Jeff: Yes.

Jim: I mean, I was in a restaurant—

Jeff: Yes.

Jim: —I told you this story years ago when a friend of mine and his late adolescent daughter, she was going with her boyfriend to a concert at a venue an hour and change from where we lived, and because the boyfriend's car was a clunker and hers was a clunker, the dad was going to let her take his relatively new car, but he was sort of deciding against it because... they weren't having a fight, they were having a conversation... and he said that he really didn't have confidence that if the boyfriend had been drinking at the concert, which is a perfectly reasonable thing for him to do, and then insisted on being the man and driving home that she would say, "No, no, no, I'll be the driver," and she then launched into a thing about how he didn't value her independence. I think this was in the form of a conversation not a screaming match...

Jeff: Yes.

Jim: And he looked at her and said, "I will know that you have achieved the kind of maturity and independence that you say you've achieved—

Jeff: Yes.

Jim: "—when we come here and I suggest you order the salmon and you have the salmon anyway."

Jeff: Un-huh, beautiful… because you want to.

Jim: Yeah, because you want to.

Jeff: Yep.

Jim: Well, because you want to and then also, for me anyway, it is also things like I don't really want to as in this is my heart's desires, but I choose to because it is important.

Jeff: Yes.

Jim: Or because it is meaningful… like that.

Jeff: Yes.

Jim: That, you know…

Jeff: Because it serves the greater good.

Jim: Right. That I want to be able to make that shift with more reliability—

Jeff: Yes.

Jim: —when…

Jeff: Yes.

Jim: And again, these are all things that are, you know, if I need to show up at church because, you know, it is an emergency or somebody is dying, or—

Jeff: You're there.

Jim: That just goes pretty much without saying.

Jeff: Right.

Jim: But for these more...

Jeff: Suddenly you are no longer on the reservation.

Jim: Right. (*Note here and in the above interchanges how often I re-spond "Right" which could also be heard by my unconscious as "Write."*)

Jeff: Yes, I understand.

Jim: Okay, I'm sorry.

Jeff: No, you're okay with that and that is a, you know, you're speaking to a universal because I am sure that each of us in the room can relate to that in our lives. I can certainly relate to that in my life and, as you are talking about that, I think of my examples and so the strength of take the line on a walk. (*Now Jeff talks to me by talking to the room as he has been talking to the room by talking to me.*)

Jim: Un-huh.

Jeff: And the absurd nature of the way in which a simple metaphor can reorganize life. Well, people die for metaphors. They die for their flag in combat...

Jim: Yeah.

Jeff: And people live for metaphors, and a simple metaphor can have a snowballing effect in ways that you can't possibly predict and certainly in ways that you shouldn't program.

Jim: Okay.

Jeff: So if the metaphor, when the metaphor has some meaning to you and you are suddenly back with your son... Steven?

Jim: Dave.

Jeff: David, and you are back with your son, David, and you are in the garage and the light is streaming into the venue...

Jim: Take a line for the walk.

Jeff: Overcome the trouble and you take the line for a walk, and then you see because there is an asymptote there, and I don't expect any of us to fully get there. There can be some residual, "I won't if I have to," and there can be some residual "No, no, no, no nuh nuh no, no nuh nuh no no, no nuh nuh no no NO no" towards serving the greater good, but it is an asymptote and every little bit, every little step, and take the line for a walk…

Jim: Okay.

Jeff: We will see where you go with that—

Jim: Okay, okay.

Jeff: —and how that reverberates, but for Christ's sake—and I mean for Christ's sake— (*Here Jeff focuses and brings my priesthood and spirituality to bear.*)

Jim: Yeah, I know you do.

Jeff: —don't make this like somebody comes up with a good idea and somebody is sure to overextend it. Somebody comes up with a good idea, and somebody comes up with a good idea and somebody else will deconstruct it.

Jim: Un-huh.

Jeff: Somebody comes up with a good idea and somebody else will overanalyze it and it would be better to just let the idea have its own orientation. (*Here, Jeff de-potentiates what often happens in the group in the short breaks between structures when we talk over what just happened.*)

Jim: Yeah, its own valence.

Jeff: Try it.

Jim: Okay.

Jeff: The concept of its own valence and see how that can reverberate into areas of life.

Jim: Okay, okay, that's good.

Jeff: So, we have just teased out, right, so a principal now— (*Talking more to the group than talking to me... Actually, this is an indirect way of talking with me.)*

Jim: Okay.

Jeff: —is to know that there is a vibrant intelligence and, that given room, that people will sometimes stumble on their vibrant intelligence and that our job can be to help them to recognize what it is and make it a little more three-dimensional, and we see that, for example, in many of the sessions that have been happening, and Marius is particularly brilliant at doing that. (*Jeff's mentioning of three dimensions harks back to my three-part laying out of what was before and between us captured in my physical gestures at the beginning of our session.*)

Jim: Yeah, he is.

Jeff: Yeah, we can pick up on some of the threads that he creates in that regard. You're no slouch. Okay. Well, that was interesting conversational hypnosis.

Jim: Thank you.

Jeff: No, thank you, because it is not something that was just for you. I will play with that too and see what that gets me in terms of serving the greater good that I want.

Jim: Okay, deal.

Jeff: Yeah, thank you.

Jim: Thank you.

Jeff: Okay, so....

Comment

As I reflect on the title to this essay, "Take a Line for a Walk," I am struck by how I metabolized the experience subsequent to the session. I find it particularly interesting that, as I began to write the first draft of this essay, I was doing so with pen and paper and not my usual keyboarding onto the computer. I am legally blind and must use a CCTV monitor to physically write. I must print the piece to have any chance of being able to read what I have written in this way. That I find handwriting arduous in the extreme not only due to my partial blindness but because of neuropathy in my fingers due to diabetes—that I began this work by literally taking a line for a walk with this pen and ink on paper. I have not used the process of handwriting for anything in at least 20 years.

While I did not run home and magically begin to work on this chapter or any other writing project, I did review the video of the session multiple times, and I read and re-read and studied the transcription of the session. It almost felt to me as if I were trying to commit it to memory. Only then did I begin to write, to take a line for a walk with pen to paper.

In closing I offer these final thoughts. When I was finishing my studies in Ericksonian Hypnotherapy and Psychotherapy at the New York Milton H. Erickson Institute, Dr. Sidney Rosen told me that first I needed to study Erickson's work, then I needed to study the work of his students, and then I needed to study my own work if I really wanted to master the craft. The Master Class has allowed me to do all three at once within a group of skilled, compassionate, dedicated, and gifted colleagues. Knowing how much we have all benefited from our time together with Jeff, I agreed to write this chapter for the collected works of the New York City Master Class so that others could experience the richness of Jeff's work.

Again, I encourage you to study and pull apart the transcript of this session, in fact all the sessions in this book, so that they, the sessions, and it, the book, are not just something you read but something with which you engage and with which you have a learning experience. Then, study your own work as well, using recordings if possible, so that you can craft and re-craft what you do with your clients. Take your own lines for a walk.

In the Deep Midwinter

Barbara Birge

One of the greatest pleasures and privileges of training in clinical hypnosis has been to experience Jeff Zeig's deep kindness, wrapped in artistry. His Master Classes, of course, afford the chance not only to receive his supervision, but also to receive his help for one's own clinical problems.

In this mode of patient, I asked for Jeff's help with my dread of winter—in particular, of early darkness and long, solitary nights. With the arrival of autumn, I would begin to suffer from melancholy as many people do. Anticipating that feeling had become an issue in itself. But in a single session during a Master Class nearly a decade ago, Jeff's work shifted my relationship with autumn and winter for all the years that have ensued. What I consciously recall is that, in my hypnotic state, he invited me into the nighttime dark of the outdoors where I experienced its deep, safe, velvet beauty. Jeff also incorporated Gestalt techniques in our work, and I seem to recall him hovering behind me, helping create the impression of being enveloped in the darkness. Physicalizing emotional experiences is one of Jeff's great talents, and I was the beneficiary.

My changed perception of the night as rich, beautiful, welcoming, and even beckoning, has remained my experience. What a remarkable gift to have received from Jeff—one that has accumulated into years of ease and the ability to savor every season.

Many thanks to a dear teacher.

CHAPTER TEN

The Utilization of Self
in the Creation of Reference Experiences

Robert Staffin

The explicit presentation of material is informative, it provides the what, why, and how of a subject. Implicit information is evocative, it triggers searches, a quest for clarity, and invites one to organize and reorganize ideas, experiences, and associations in new ways. Talking about the former is easy; conveying the latter is more of a challenge. A Master Class with Dr. Jeffrey K. Zeig contains both elements.

I have grappled with how best to capture the essence of what it is like to work with Jeff: the gestures he uses to enhance his message, the way he uses his voice to emphasize ideas, his ability to play with words creating confusion, shock, and surprise with double entendres, puns, analogies, and metaphors. All of these pale, however, when I note the compassion, the warmth, and the sensitivity in which he packages the strategic intent of the therapeutic encounter.

As we know, Jeff is a prolific and respected author, a speaker, a psychologist, an internationally renowned master therapist, and yet, this man literally lay on the floor in front of me, ostensibly to access an experiential sense of my impatience but more probably to help me cultivate a different relationship with that part of myself.

The session transcribed here is from the master class that took place in NYC in January of 2015.

The Utilization of Self
in the Creation of Reference Experiences

J: Welling up...

R: Percolating...

J: Percolating...

R: And I got to tell you, just being here, being with you guys in and of itself is soothing and healing.

J: Great.

R: I'm off to a good start.

J: Well good for you for being open to the ambient effect.

R: It's one of the joys of coming actually.

J: Well, what would be the ambient effect? Would it be adventure? Would it be chill? Would it be—

R: It's love.

J: Love.

R: It's just safe. Be who you are: explore, enjoy, learn, grow, develop, test.

J: Mm-hmm.

R: But it's all done, it's just held so tenderly and securely. (*Note how this idea of holding gets picked up and developed.*)

J: Tender and secure is really good and tender and secure could be a launching place for getting many good places.

R: But I need to give you a little more of what's been going on.

J: Yeah.

I summarize the recent loss of my beloved father-in-law, some issues with my parents, and the respective statuses of my grown children.

R: So I'm in a vulnerable spot and yet there have been a handful of times in my life where I have been in similar spots and I am tremendously confident that it is just the beginning of the next blossoming. (*With my arms raised up.*)

J: Okay.

I speak about an upcoming board exam, why I have pursued it, and what it means to me, and my fears. Jeff summarizes this with the phrase, "Welcome to the fraternity."

J: Although, it's still about vulnerability. (*This is an example of Jeff's ability to note and track a theme, e.g., my concerns about passing the exam and being accepted into the "fraternity" are an expression of vulnerability.*)

R: Yeah, right.

J: Okay, so if I were holding (*Jeff leans forward with his hands cupped*) your vulnerability…

R: By the way, that's just one of the many things I love about you.

J: Mm-hmm.

R: The capacity to just distill it down and say (*mirroring Jeff's gesture*) "There it is."

J: Right. So if I were holding your vulnerability—(*Jeff looks down into his cupped hands and nonverbally invites me to join him. I accept the invitation.*)—what would it be like? What would be the shape? The color? The texture? (*This is Jeff fleshing out my experience so that he can increase his impact by using my words, metaphors, gestures, and descriptors.*)

R: It's almost like the thing in *Eraserhead*. Just sort of this "euwgh." Not that I think about *Eraserhead* very often.

J: Uh-huh, but that was the first thing that came to your mind.

R: (*Chuckling.*) There it was.

J: Uh-huh.

R: Squirming in your hands.

J: Uh-huh. Is it squirming?

R: It was. It's raw, it's vulnerable, it's just new to the world. It's cold. It's sensitive to the subtlest shifts of the currents in the room. It's, it's vulnerable.

J: Because there's nothing to insulate it and protect it so it's... Even the slightest touch, even the slightest movement can cause it to squirm.

R: (*Staring at Jeff holding my vulnerability.*) Mm-hmm.

J: So now, as you look at your vulnerability, how can you begin to honor it, appreciate it? (*This is the beginning of Jeff assisting me in altering my relationship to/with my vulnerability, a reframe for which he later gives me credit as he labels my stance "Gilliganesque," referring to Steve Gilligan.*)

R: I've got a blanket. (*I wipe away tears.*)

J: That would be insulation.

R: Actually, I've got a swatch of my blanket and you know me right, everything comes with a story.

J: Yes.

R: I was very attached to my blanket.

J: Uh-huh.

R: And my mother got very concerned and asked the pediatrician, "At what point should we take it away?"

J: Uh-huh.

R: And he said... "Just before he walks down the aisle." (*Jeff and group laugh.*)

J: Great pediatrician.

R: So, at our rehearsal dinner, my mom gave me my blanket.

J: Uh-huh.

R: Yeah, it's hard to be mad at that lady you know?

J: Uh-huh.

R: And my dad, when I was talking with him about how upset I was about the decisions they've made recently, he said, "You know, there was this phenomenal French architect and he made these bridges in the city of Paris that the people just loved to cross and phenomenal buildings that were so ornate and beautiful. The inside was even richer than the outside."

J: Uh-huh.

R: "And one day he got caught sucking off some guy and he became known as Pierre the cocksucker."

J: (*Laughing.*) That was what your dad said?

R: (*Nods.*)

J: All's fair in met - a - phor. (*Laughter in the room.*)

R: So that's my stock, you know?

J: Uh-huh. So now that I've got your vulnerability, where did it come from?

This is an example of Jeff's sensitivity. He knows who I am, allows me to communicate something that is important to me via my use of stories. He accepts my digressions, and then returns to my experience of vulnerability. His having consistently done this over the years we have worked together is part of what promotes my trust and confidence in him and leaves me available to follow his leads.

J: Where did we take this from in your body?

R: (*Pauses.*) You know, it just feels like it comes out of my guts.

J: Right, okay. So now considering your encyclopedic knowledge of music (*utilization*), what music would accompany your vulnerability?

Pause.

R: There's a song called "Box of Rain." "And it's just a box of rain. I don't know who put it there. Believe it if you need it or leave it if you dare, for it's just a box of rain, full of ribbons for your hair. Such a long long time to be gone and a short time to be there."

J: Giving you time to feel your way into the sense of your own metaphor. (*Jeff has no idea what this means to me but he is, nonetheless, permissive.*)

R: There is a line in that song, "Inch your way through dead dreams to another land." And I feel like that's what I am in the process of doing.

J: (*Nodding.*) Entering a new stage of life, a different stage (*I nod*) with your parents, with your children, with Gail, with Gail's parents... And you want this to accompany you. (*Attention to language—Jeff, having invited me to identify some music to accompany my vulnerability now weaves the language of music and into the tapestry of life.*)

R: That's an essential piece... while in relation to it, with it.

J: Right.

R: I resonate fully.

J: Right. Okay, so take it for a moment—(*Jeff, who has been holding my vulnerability this whole time, now offers it to me, who place my hands below Jeff's to accept my vulnerability*)—and just resonate with it. It's going to accompany you into this next stage of life and perhaps it needs to hear the rhythm of that song so that it can begin to evolve itself into a way that is fitting with this stage of who Rob is. (*Reframes vulnerability as evolutionary.*)

Looking down into the palms of my cupped hands, I comment on my deteriorated visual acuity and my associations to me unconventional wedding ring.

R: And it defies the convention of Judaism of having a solid band. And I've thought, "Oh, there's a couple of conventions I've defied over the years, that's okay." But what I like about it is the way that it's woven. And that there's a strength and within the strength there are holes and space and it's...

J: Slow down a little so that you can feel the sense of what you are saying. It's beautiful. (*There is a double entendre here: what I am saying is beautiful and the ring is beautiful.*) It's woven. I'm woven.

R: And it's un—

J: It's defiant. I'm defiant.

R: It's not perfect.

J: That's a good one too.

R: So—

J: It's not necessarily in focus and it does not have necessarily to be in focus.

R: Excuse me. (*I reach past Jeff for a tissue and wipe my eyes and nose.*)

J: And yes, the wear and tear of time has a way of tarnishing momentarily the insulation. (*Note the language again, the parallel between gold metal and tarnish.*) And the function of your vulnerability in the next manifestation of who Rob will be.... may not be in focus, may not be clear, doesn't need to be clear at this point. (*Jeff utilizing the properties of metal, my declining visual acuity, my vision being blurred by tears and my transitional state.*)

R: There are certainly familiar steps that are helpful.

J: Mm-hmm.

R: Simply being kind, and that can grow out of my own vulnerability. There's nothing inconsistent in the world with that but...

J: So as you take time and you magnify the realization of time and that can be kind certainly to your parents and kind to Leah and kind to Josh and kind to Gail and most important, it's being kind to Rob. And that's the font from which the other kindness has its own generativity. So if your vulnerability as your vulnerability is being kind to you right now, what does your vulnerability communicate, in a moment of kindness? (*Jeff now leans forward again holding my vulnerability in his hands.*)

R: I appreciate the warmth and the softness with which you hold me and although I remain tender and sensitive I know I am safe. (*A poignant example of the unconscious speaking about its experience of this present encounter with Jeff, what one could label "an interactional double entendre."*)

J: You can imagine your vulnerability as having a resonance (*Jeff hums*) and energy (*he hums again*). You could imagine that resonant energy as if that resonant energy was an induction (*Jeff hums again*).

R: It would be a lower pitch. (*Jeff hums at a lower pitch. He is communicating the message "I'm here, I'm listening, and I'm responsive."*)

I speak about my experience at an Al Pesso (founder of Pesso Boyden System Psychotherapy) workshop and my realization about my desire to get things just right.

R: So the first resonance was too high, I'm sorry. (*I clasp Jeff's hands that are still holding my vulnerability.*)

J: It's okay, I know you want to get it in the way that you want it. (*Profoundly accepting.*)

R: Yeah, I can probably just…

J: And you can use your imagination and imagine that your vulnerability is creating an induction for your heart, as if your vulnerability were resonating.

R: It's more like an "Ohm."

J: Okay, tremendous.

R: There's a… there's almost a heartbeat, a harmonic resonance.

J: Bah bum, bah bum… Can we get a Jim baritone? Bah bum… (*Jeff utilizes Jim, my dear friend and Master Class partner in crime. Jim, off camera, is heard, "Bah bum, Bah bum." Chuckles in the room.*)

R: It's at a good distance too.

J: And Ohm. (*Jim is heard intoning, "Ohm."*)

J: So that you can feel it in your heart and it's the kind (*double entendre—kind, as kindness, and kind, as in type*) of resonance that you can appreciate and the kind of resonance that you can begin to allow and appreciate. Enjoy with all of it tones and undertones and overtones (*Jeff alters the tone and location of his voice as he mentions these different kinds of tones*).

R: I want to experience it more in my core, not my heart, to let it emanate from that center.

J: Go for it. How are you doing that?

R: I'll let you know when I get there.

J: Take your time.

R: Don't wait for me. Maybe you can help me get there.

J: Core concepts, core ideas, core realizations and that there's a wellspring in your history, a magical (*I write a daily missive entitled "Your Daily Dose of Magic"*) core experience. So that you can go into the repository and explore the repository of core.

R: And very quickly two things come to mind, two experiences. One was the time we had the class at Susan's.

J: Yep.

R: You had me do that evolution of man (*with eyes closed, I gesture with my right arm in a bouncing movement*) and I just remember sitting on the floor at one point just sobbing with just an awareness of the compassion and the pain in the world and just feeling so grateful that I could experience that and be aware of that and feel that. And then another time here with Caroline as my therapist where I had that same feeling, and I remember somebody gave me a tissue and I was like, "No, you don't understand. This is good. Leave me alone. I don't get here a lot." (*I wave off the people I recall offering me a tissue*).

J: Mm-hmm.

R: So when I think about my reference points, those are two of, two of the good ones.

J: Oceanic feelings. (*Jeff's capacity to sum things up speaks to his intelligence and communicates a sense of truly being with the other.*)

R: Yeah.

J: So how is your vulnerability creating that core induction? (*Implied causative.*)

R: As we were speaking and the tears begin to flow, I don't experience it as the vulnerability I'm holding out here (*I gesture to the space between me and Jeff*) or the vulnerability I'm cultivating in here, it's just allowing myself to experience what I'm talking with you about, what I'm describing, not you know, "I think this and I think that." (*I point to my head and wag it from side to side as I state "this" and "that"*) just feeling the—

J: Well, if you wanted to, could you get impatient with yourself? (*This is a transition point in the session. Why did he bring impatience in? Jeff is utilizing our relationship and his knowledge of who I am.*)

R: (*Laughs.*) You're cheating, you know I can.

J: And, what greater good would that serve?

R: Well, I can take the question seriously or I can take the question as a paradoxical "And if you discover... (*I gesture to my right with my arm arching from above my shoulder out to my right.*)

J: Yes. Both/and is good.

R: The bigger challenge is taking it more literally.

J: Mm-hmm.

R: (*Nodding.*)

J: And I would want to believe that it serves a greater good, in the sense that Santayana, the philosopher, said, "That somebody comes up with a good idea somebody else is sure to overextend it."

R: I kind of lost the question. What's the greater good of my being impatient with myself? What greater good does that serve?

J: (*Nodding.*) Play with it. You don't have come up with the... You don't have to impatiently (*now he is seeding*) come up with the right answer.

R: (*I chortle.*)

J; There could be some... there could be a takeaway here.

R: Okay.

J: Okay, so now, as you explore the essential human vulnerability of passages of life and children and moving on, going into a new stage—(*Jeff is summarizing what I have presented in a more implicit manner: my father-in-law died, my daughter will be graduating from college, I had been speaking about my relationship with my parents*)—and the fraternity and whether or not they will welcome you—(*I had expressed concern about my upcoming board exam, which Jeff framed as admittance into a fraternity*)—

R: (*Nodding.*) And that you know, just the way you say that...

J: Mm-hmm.

R: Without even the examples of it...

J: Mm-hmm.

R: You know, it wells up in... (*inaudible*).

J: Well, it wells up in your eyes.

R: (*Chuckle.*) The minute that came out of my mouth. (*Laughing.*)

J: Right.

R: It's a sensitivity. Its just a... there's a permissiveness to be, just be. It's okay. That feels really good—(*I have arrived at that place of compassion to which I had made reference earlier*)—and it's also like okay, (*looking up, gesturing with my hands out at chest level, palms up, and with a tear-choked voice*) and why don't I do it more often?

J: Well, and you got impatient with yourself again.

R: Okay, fair enough, but not in a way that would block it.

J: Uh-huh. I have a collection of Buddhas, because they represent different things and one of them is the compassionate Buddha. Do you have any image of the compassionate Buddha?

R: I would make one up. I don't know the... I've got happy Buddha in my head.

J: Right, yes.

R: I can imagine a sorrowful Buddha.

J: The compassionate Buddha that I have is in the lotus position like totally folded in on himself. (*Jeff mimics this posture, leaning forward and placing his closed fists against his forehead with his elbows resting on his knees.*)

R: Yeah.

J: And that is a unique and ubiquitous image of the compassionate Buddha. I couldn't see it when I first encountered it.

R: I don't know if you remember the time at Susan's apartment but that was the posture that I was in.

J: (*Nods.*)

R: And felt the weight... on my back, everywhere... I don't know if that was the...

J: I didn't have a conscious recollection.

R: (*Laughing.*) Cause I couldn't find the word I was looking for.

J: Okay, and so you experience that and you have hooked yourself to Jim who operationalizes that in a way that is peerless.

R: (*Nodding.*) And again, just you know, simply hearing that and then being aware of it, you know, I know it.

J: Right.

R: And I feel it.

J: Right.

R: And forget it.

J: Right. The metaphor is that health is the ability to recuperate. So you're not healthy because you avoid disease. Everybody steps in shit. Everybody gets a cold, nice recovery (*Jeff gestures with his arm being knocked down and popping back up like a Bobo doll to represent recuperation*) and I wouldn't want to walk around all day like a compassionate Buddha. I'd like to go to a football game and experience something different. So the accessibility of that is how you call up what program you need. (*Jeff is seeding for the importance of being more than a one-trick pony, a part of reframing impatience.*)

R: So a friend of mine was teaching a morning yoga class on mindfulness and meditation and it was at a good time, 7:30 in the morning, and I could go there before I started my day.

J: You could go there?

R: Yes. And I thought this is delightful.

J: Mm-hmm.

R: I could do this because I do that and then it's like having the exam.

J: Yeah, right, okay, so we did this thing last... in March last year. (*Jeff is referencing a piece of work we did around a private, sensitive matter. That he can do this in this setting without violating my confidence is impressive; that he aligns himself with me and models a path for change is masterful.*)

R: Yeah, not a problem.

J: Well, not a problem for me either. I think we did that on Thursday. It was the first day or the second day of the seminar that we were... you were waffling about the decision in your life and I said okay, you know we're brothers, let's put something, each of us put something on the table, and that morning I had been listening to Dan Amen as I was exercising downstairs and he's going, "No sugar, no sugar, no sugar," and I'm thinking, "No sugar," this is ridiculous, you know, I couldn't do that. And then it came to this idea of being a brother with you and putting something on the table and we were both going to do that together and this is certainly in the purview of "Why not just give the patient an assignment and the therapist an assignment that's a good thing" and step up you know also because we're in this model of growth and development. (*Jeff is simultaneously talking with me and teaching, and modeling for the group dimensions of being a psychotherapist.*)

R: And there are few people in the world that I would be willing to do that with. (*This is my implicit granting license to Jeff and inviting more, something I trust he knows already.*)

J: Right, I appreciate that, so that fit for us. It was not—

R: Right.

J: —necessarily going to be the case with anybody else. It fit for us but I know you from so many sessions so I knew that it would fit. But the most amazing thing was the next morning when I woke up, absolutely unexpected to me, my identity changed. And suddenly it just popped into place, "I am a person who doesn't eat desserts. I don't eat sugar," and it was an amazingly shocking moment. I absolutely didn't expect that to happen. I knew that willfully I could carry out the plan but I didn't expect that suddenly there would be that shift and it's completely carried on and I like it. So it's worked. (*Seeding by telling the story of positive change and then moving on to my impatience.*) Now let's operationalize for a moment your impatience with yourself. Right? If we could operationalize your vulnerability and put that here (*leaning in towards me with hands cupped as before*), give me your impatience with yourself and help me to operationalize that and feel that.

R: (*Throws his impatience to the ground.*) You'll have to pick it up because it's over there.

J: Uh-huh and okay (*Jeff mimics the throwing gesture*), so it's aggressive.

R: Yeah.

J: Right... zzzpt. If there were a sound...

R: THWAP!

J: Thwap.

R: That's hitting the ground and...

J: Right and it makes a puddle. (*Laughter in the room.*)

R: It's a little more viscous than that, it's, it's, it's more like...

J: Silly putty?

R: Well, it's, it's, it's... (*smacking my forehead and chuckling to myself*)—sorry. By the way when I gave myself the Rorschach—

J: Uh-huh.

R: —you don't want to know how many responses I offered. (*Laughing.*)

J: Too many little Ds. Uh-huh.

R: Woo hoo. Very experiential.

J: You know better now.

R: (*Cracking up, followed by others joining in on the laughter.*) Touché.

J: So, excuse me (*Jeff speaking to my impatience on the floor*) Rob's impatience, here you are—

R: "What the fuck do you want?"

J: —on the ground. You know suddenly, "Whoop," (*with throwing gesture*) and there you are...

R: Are you done yet?

J: What, what the fuck are you doing there? And, ah, what's the story? And yeah, I suppose that in the same way I would want to know how do you serve the greater good?

R: (*Looking up and enacting the impatience on the floor, I say in a fainter, slightly startled and woozy voice:*) It's a little hard from down here. Now it's just sort of kind of, "Huh, what happened to me?" It's still a little loopy from the throw, you know.

J: Yeah, okay.

R: It's like Gumby, you know, it's going to reconstitute itself "Zzuup." Claymation—it's back up. (*I gesture with my hands palms up moving my arms from my belly up to the space before my chest.*) Get back to work.

J: Get back to work.

R: And it's not work, "Go see patients." It's not work, "Go study work." It's just, you know, "Go on, will you?"

J: Yeah.

R: What's next?

J: Uh-huh. Well, you know in my own, like if you were doing little D's, I would do experiential, be a little absurd so do you mind if I just slip into the "Zlppt" that's down there?

R: Knock yourself out. But be careful because it's reconstituted.

J: (*Lying on the floor to my right.*) I can reconstitute. (*Suddenly Jeff jerks up off the floor, arms and legs lifting.*) "Blurp!" (*Laughter in the room.*) All right.

R: (*Leaning over to look down at Jeff on the floor.*) See now, if Jim would do that for me, it would really mean something. (*Laughter.*)

J: (*In an "I'm melting" kind of voice.*) "Oh no."

Jim: You rang?

R: No, no, no.

J: Okay, so here I am.

Jim: Don't make me come in there.

J: Here I am. I am stuck here and I'm intense and I'm powerful.

R: Well, actually, you're not.

J: I can.

R: Sorry, you're really not. (*Jeff, in response to my deflating him, raises his head up off of the floor and stares at me.*)

J: No.

R: No, bad news. You're kind of in shock.

J: "Boop." (*And lays back down.*)

R: How did I get here?

J: Uh-huh.

R: And what happened to my arms? And I've lost my voice and... but wait a second, it's starting to come... I'm getting reoriented.

J: Yeah, I can reconstitute. (*Malicious laughter.*)

R: Now you're gettin' it.

J: Uh-huh, yeah.

R: And then you can just kind of pop back up, but you don't have to. I'd be happy for you to, you could if you want.

J: Right, okay, so what form do I take when I pop back up? I need to have a little vision here.

R: I mean it's gremlinesque.

J: Uh-huh, yeah.

R: And just...

J: (*Raising his hands so that they appear gnarled.*) Ah ha ha!

R: (*High pitched.*) Eh he he, eh he he.

J: "Eh he he," uh-huh. (*In a deep, husky voice.*) People, people...

R: Don't fuck with me, cowboy, because I can make your life miserable.

J: Uh huh, yeah, okay. Well, there we go. I can get there.

R: Yeah.

J: (*Lying on the floor gestures and grumbles to himself.*)

R: It's not a wicked witch you know, it's playful but watch your ass.

J: Uh-huh, yeah, uh-huh. (*Raising his head off of the floor.*) Ya ha ha ha!

R: (*Laughing.*) Yeah, you can get there! (*Laughter in the room.*) Yeah, uh-huh. I think I've created a monster!

J: Okay, so, I'm just waiting here to reconstitute and do my "eh ha ha ha." (*Laughter in the room.*) Gotchya! (*Lifts his head from the floor looking at me up in the chair.*) "Ah ha ha ha ha!" (*There's laughter in the room, as I am looking down at my feet, smiling, and nodding my head. Jeff, on his back on the floor, looks from the ceiling over to me, sitting on his right.*) Well, hanging out, "Ah ha ha ha ha!" (*Jeff, lying on the floor, plays with his sweater, shows his belly.*)

R: It's a little hard to take you seriously now. (*Jeff, by enacting my impatience, has caused me to experience and relate to my impatience in a different way.*)

J: Uh-huh.

R: So...

J: (*In a somewhat mechanical voice:*) "Abner Doubleday, you just invented baseball. Don't take the world serious." (*Jeff may be animating the Abner Doubleday character to convey the message not to take the world so seriously.*)

R: I don't remember who it was but in the first day we were talking and we were saying, "You know, it's better than TV, you can reach out and touch it."

J: (*Still lying on the ground.*) Yeah, well, I don't know because I was morphing back and forth and I was becoming...

R: I'm sorry Dr. Zeig, but if you are going to be Dr. Zeig you've got to get off the floor. (*This is something Jeff has taught; when one is enacting or has someone enacting a role and they begin to respond as themselves or editorialize as opposed to maintaining the role they are enacting, he points it out.*)

J: Yeah well, I was morphing back and forth and I was thinking okay, if it was me and I was sitting in the chair, I'd put my foot on it. If it was me and I was sitting in the chair I'd have Jim sit on it... Don't do that (*directed to Jim*). Right, because I think that the essential part of this is that you don't get to... You know, like I am an anti-evolutionary force.

R: And you know, I like the word that has been floating in the class this time around... authenticity.

J: Mm-hmm.

R: And you know for me being authentic with that part is cultivating a relationship with it. (*Jeff had seeded this idea earlier.*)

J: (*Rising from the floor and returning to his chair across from me:*) Yes, that will be Gilliganesque—cultivate a relationship with it and honor it and be open to it and accept it and it would be no different than saying to a 400-pound man, "You need to accept where you are before you lose the first pound." It would be something that you would know and that you would operationalize (*Jeff laying out a roadmap*) for anybody else and you know your tendency is, "Oh my god, Thwap!" is going to get in the way of you cultivating your vulnerability and your compassion. It's an anti-evolutionary force. (*Jeff is fleshing out the reference that my impatience is something that interferes with my willingness to be vulnerable and my desire to be compassionate.*)

R: Have you been rethinking all parts have value? (*This is an idea Jeff has also had.*)

J: All parts have value.

R: Have you?

J: The value: it keeps you young...

R: (*Laughs.*)

J: (*Leaning over towards where he was lying on the floor as my impatience.*) "Excuse me, do you want your blankey?" (*Referenced earlier in the session.*)

R: You confused me with that because I wouldn't have offered a blanket—

J: Blankey. (*Interrupting and using the more childish word perhaps to make it more ego dystonic.*)

R: I still wouldn't offer a blanket to that little fucker. "Get your own blanket." So, it's reconstituted. That's it.

J: Mm-hmm. Well, you know, what if we send your impatience to the Rock 'n' Roll Museum in Cleveland (*here Jeff is utilizing my love of music and propensity to communicate ideas using song lyrics*) and just leave it there for a while? It can be with any other artifact that you would find in the museum.

R: (*Laughing.*) Have you ever been to Cleveland?

J: No.

R: The Cuyahoga river, the only river in America that burns. (*Jeff and I laugh.*) Sending it away doesn't feel right.

J: Mm-hmm.

R: It's not that I need it, but I need to cultivate a relationship with it. As opposed to—

J: Yes.

R: —bash it.

J: So help me to see you do that. I'll step back a little bit so you… (*Jeff sliding his chair back after having looked down at where the impatience was lying. I look down at it and begin to address it.*)

R: Dude, you gotta relax. Um.

J: Now you are instructing it so let's get to the purifying stage and the acceptance stage and…

R: Are we in a rush?

J: What?

R: Are we in a rush?

J: No, it seemed like you were in a rush, that you were pushing, that you were going to step 3 before you went to step 2.

R: It's an opening gambit. (*I whisper this conspiratorially to Jeff.*)

J: I'm sorry?

R: It's an opening gambit.

J: Oh, I see.

R: Shhh, don't tell anybody.

J: (*Raises his index finger to his lips indicating silence.*)

R: So, um, I need to understand what's gonna work for you... Well, I'll tell you, what works for me is being able to take that breath and just step back because you've watched the number of times I've come back into the room and said, "I acted rashly." (*Sobering.*) You know, I feel your presence, there are those times where, you know, I'm trying to figure something out and it's stupid stuff, like how to download something into QuickBooks, and Gail comes in or the kids come in and I'm just... (*My shoulders begin to quiver.*) "Leave me alone." (*I look up and whisper something to Jeff who first shakes his head no and then nods yes. I redirect my gaze to the floor.*) The kids are growing up. They're out of the house for the most part. It's a time to take stock and see where you're going and how you're going to spend this time, and you've helped me get through a lot of stuff. And I don't want to get rid of you, but I'd like to develop the type of relationship with you where you can trust that... ah, you know, I can attend to the vulnerability and you're not gonna stop smacking me if I step too far over the line but... ah maybe we'll get you one of those bands that a physical therapist would send you home with to exercise a particular muscle, different colors for different strengths of resistance. We could just put your hands at your waist, attached to that band. If you could get it up there hard enough quick enough against the resistance, well, then maybe I deserve to get smacked. (*Looking up from the floor to Jeff.*) But otherwise, slow down, Cowboy.

J: I'm wondering if Cowboy would also have a way of tutoring you to develop your compassion. (*The question is intended to facilitate the evolution of my impatience.*)

R: (*Now whispering to Cowboy on the floor.*) That's the problem, it doesn't happen that fast.

J: No.

R: I was responding to him.

J: Yeah.

R: Tutoring me on how to what my compassion?

J: How to evolve (*Jeff gestures enlarging it with his hands*) your compassion.

R: Um.

J: I was feeling sorry for him because just doing "Ah ha ha ha" was just you know, well, that's a one-trick pony. (*Jeff is modeling compassion towards my impatience as an indirect model for me towards myself.*)

R: Well, I don't know that he's the best tutor, you know?

J: I don't either. That's why I wonder if. We're just exploring as brothers: where can be the greater good? (*Jeff's characterization of brothers is something that he knows will appeal to me thus making the idea to explore my relationship to my impatience more appealing and compelling.*)

R: (*Sitting in a contemplative, post-trance stillness.*) I'm at a loss.

J: Food for thought... I'm with you 172% about the acceptance factor and being with your impatience, and maybe in the Wei-Kai moment, this impatience, this is not my impatience. (*Wei-Kei is a class participant who led another student through a series of this x is not my x.*)

R: (*Smiling.*) I wasn't sure if that was an invitation to play that.

J: Mm-hmm.

I look at my impatience on the floor and then sit up straight, close my eyes, and Jeff begins.

J: And as a mindfulness exercise, as if you are watching your impatience—(*Jeff, even though my eyes are closed, gestures with his right hand moving from right to left like an image moving across a screen*)—and it's squirming (*referencing the initial description of vulnerability, which I borrowed from the movie* Eraserhead) and dancing and "pfsssting" (*gestures it being thrown to the ground*) and morphing and you're just mindfully watching, "Oh, this impatience is not my impatience." (*Jeff, who had been gesturing left to right with one arm as he offered the "scenes," now gestures expansively with both arms as he employs the mantra "this impatience is not my impatience."*)

R: (*Smiling and nodding.*) I can see, it's almost like in the movie Ghost where the character steps out, you can see it coming out of the character. (*I too am gesturing with my arm, representing a trailing movement.*)

J: Right.

R: This impatience is not my impatience.

J: Right, right.

R: And then having another incarnation of impatience and... (*I move from slumped to upright with a gesture of the next iteration of impatience moving up and through me only to be delivered out onto the floor again.*) This impatience is not my impatience. (*Opening my eyes and looking at Jeff.*) Like Sisyphus! (*Laughing.*) This impatience is not my impatience. And this impatience, and this... (*Rolling my head with each iteration of this phrase.*)

J: Right (*nodding*), we're back to little Ds.

R: (*Nodding and with a smile growing on my face.*) I'm smiling at the reassurance that I don't need to worry about your dotage. (*Both smile and chuckle.*)

J: Thanks.

R: (*Laughing.*) I feel better already.

J: Mm-hmm.

R: Okay.

J: And that would be okay, it would be like a gentleness (*his hand swirling like a slow, gentle whirlpool off of his right shoulder*), it would be an acceptance. It would be a more mindful moment. (*The expansive gesture, both hands rising palms up.*)

R: Oh, and I see it.

J: Not in the sense of rejecting. Not in the sense of externalizing.

R: I see it as becoming playful and a joke within the family. (*Jeff nodding.*)

J: Yes.

R: Where I've enlisted the kids. I've enlisted Gail and there's a gesture that simply says (*I make the gesture that threw impatience to the floor but in a slower, calmer way*), "So, whose impatience is that?"

J: (*Continuing to gently nod.*) Yeah. (*Ratifying as if to say, "Yes, go on."*)

R: It's certainly not mine.

J: Uh-huh.

R: Yeah, that works.

J: Charming! (*A ratification by Jeff implying, "I knew you could do it." I nod.*) Because you want to take your processing unit and be writing new programs for compassion. And you don't want to have background programs that are getting in the way. And that, you know, to me was, you know my dad was a wonderful charming guy who delivered the mail on the West side and took the elevated subway on a daily basis to go to the central post office and practiced sorting the mail in our apartment in the Bronx. Just a really nice guy. And he was like a first-stage booster. And he could get me off of the launching pad. Then I intuitively sought out Erickson and Viktor Frankl and Whittaker and Satir, and a whole host of people who could help me to aspire to my orbit. You could appreciate the booster. (*Jeff subtly gestures to impatience on the floor.*)

R: (*Nodding.*) I know the moment that I fell in love with you.

J: (*Smiling*) Mm-hmm.

R: You were working with S. "My father was a less than forthright businessman."

J: Uh-huh.

R: And you told multiple stories of fathers, including having met the Archbishop of Canton.

J: Ah, yeah. (*Nodding.*)

R: I was like, "Holy shit!" I gotta spend more time with this guy. (*Chuckle.*)

J: Uh-huh, he's in there, the archbishop.

R: Uh-huh, "Pray for China." (*This is what Jeff reported that the Archbishop of China had said when Jeff was expressing his gratitude to the archbishop and asking what he could do for him. The Archbishop, who had been imprisoned by the Chinese, responded, "Pray for China."*)

J: Yeah, I was invited to do a commencement speech and talked about my experience with Dominic Tang, the Archbishop of Canton, an indelible reference experience. (*This can be a parallel allusion to his lying on the floor being an indelible reference experience for me.*)

R: As have you been for me.

J: Hmm?

R: As you have been for me. Which I think I've told you each time I see you but...

J: It's all about love; the universal solvent. And whatever form that takes, spiritual love, maternal love, erotic love, paternal love, so, compassionate love… It's all about love. And the target is there. (*The session begins and ends with "love." This is an example of the elegance of Jeff's work as he looks to offer a complete gift, wrapped and tied with an attractive bow.*)

R: Targets.

J: Targets… I'm good, are you okay?

R: I'm good.

J: I'm a little tired, so great, thanks so much. It's really a pleasure. I'm really blessed to have you in my life.

R: Igualmente.

Commentary

What defines a master class is the master who teaches it. Be it music, the martial arts, or psychotherapy, how teachers convey what they have come to discover about their craft or art form is a manifestation of their mastery; how the master appreciates the students and responds to them, including who they are and what they bring to the encounter, is central to this mastery. Tailoring intervention specifically to the other so as to enhance the likelihood of his or her being impacted by the encounter is yet another dimension. Appreciating that the other will imbue the interchange with a personal meaning is also key. This chapter was written as a testament to the ways in which Jeff's mastery has touched me—and beyond that to inspire others.

The structure of Jeff's language, how he employs the paraverbal elements of communication, how he monitors and tracks the impact of his communications, the ways in which he enhances the impact of his words with movements and gestures, the authenticity and genuineness of his relatedness—all of this and more are integral to the teaching and learning. Feeling the emotional tenor, the visceral responsiveness, and the sheer joy of creative healing add to the experience.

Jeff defines himself as "an experiential psychotherapist." What I have come to understand this to mean is that he believes experience is the mutative element in the therapeutic process. Take, for example, the experience of a hypnotically induced arm levitation. The classic suggestion effect of the arm having lifted without conscious volitional intent must be reconciled with the subject's irrefutable experience of the arm having lifted. It is in the person's process of reconciling these experiences that the opportunity to be freed from self-limiting conscious beliefs and perceptions occurs.

One of the many things I have learned from Jeff is the creation and utilization of reference experiences. We have all had both positive and negative ones. When a friend says, "Remember that time when we…" and you immediately recall the time, the moment, the occurrence being evoked, we define this as a reference experience. As clinicians, we are free to use reference experiences as we work with our clients. We can draw upon aspects of our clients' histories to highlight their reference experiences. We are also able to create and structure reference experiences with and for them.

Over the course of my work with Jeff, I have gone spelunking in the lair of nagging concern, my 6-year-old self has had an audience with the Dali Lama, and I have experienced myself moving through the epochs depicted in the evolution of man illustration. In this most recent session, Jeff, ostensibly to get his own experiential sense of what it feels like to be my discarded impatience, got up out of his chair and lay supine on the floor. Take a pause to consider… Dr. Jeffrey K. Zeig, internationally renowned psychologist, lecturer, author, teacher, is lying on the floor in order to be of service to me. Yes, by having me coach him about how to be my impatience, he developed an experiential sense out of which he could further craft and hone his intervention, but more than that, he knew what meaning this gesture, in and of itself, would have for me. Although he did not know the particulars, he knew that I would imbue it with a personalized significance. It is this utilization of his understanding of me that inspires his utilization of himself to create yet another reference experience.

The title I have chosen for this chapter, the utilization of self in the creation of reference experiences, alludes to how Jeff utilized himself in a literal sense and also to who he is in my personal cosmology. The latter is what gave the session its meaning and power.

Another dimension of Jeff's mastery is the seamless way that he weaves elements of his intervention into manageable takeaways. Elegance and artistry go just so far. This is psychotherapy. It is not cleverness or wit that counts, it is the person feeling altered, whether empowered or sensing a course of action that feels doable as a result of the encounter. In the session transcribed, it is how the relationship with his impatience is transformed into the game that he will introduce to his family that is a prime example of this kind of takeaway.

When I first began studying with Jeff, I would listen to the tapes of our sessions, at times transcribing them so that I could study the structure of his language and suggestions. I shared this with him one time and he casually made reference to the fact that he never listened to the tapes of his work with Dr. Erickson. I immediately stopped listening to my tapes. The analysis of this session is an exception in the service of sharing the artistry of the master.

There is an elegance to Jeff's work. Subtle words, deeds, gestures, and orchestrations fly beneath the conscious radar. For example, in the opening of this session Jeff frames the expressed pleasure of being in the class as the "ambient effect," offering praise for being open and inquiring into the nature of this pleasure. I respond, "It's love." At the close of the session, as I am expressing my gratitude to Jeff, Jeff responds, "It's all about love, the universal solvent." This placement of bookends frames and packages the experience in a way that promotes its being available on the shelves of my experiential library.

Helen Adrienne

In the Beginning (and Middle)

Something important changed inside me as I navigated 100 hours of didactic training and subsequent practice of Ericksonian Hypnosis. I am a dedicated student. I work hard to master whatever I study. It is important to me to feel connected to and reliant on my intelligence.

My learning style remained the same when it came to cognitively studying hypnotic principles. Likewise, when it came to applications, at first I consulted scripts to learn how masters approached using hypnosis with various issues. After 20 years as a practicing therapist, however, I wasn't simply applying this new tool in my work as I always had—the dedicated and cautious student—I was overjoyed to discover that I could let go! I could feel, sense, be creative, and most glorious of all, I could trust myself to serve my patients in new and more profound ways. In the process, it felt so much easier to be me.

All of this began to take place before I met Jeff. The path to feeling transformed had gained such momentum, I knew I wanted more guidance. In 2001, I signed up for the advanced workshop in Phoenix with Jeff. Turns out, I loved his method of teaching, and on a whim, I sent him a letter when I got home asking if he would provide supervision in New York City if I assembled a group of therapists. To my surprise and delight, he agreed.

In typical Jeff style, he rattled off the requirements: 12 people, over the course of 4 days, from 9 AM to 5 PM. Before the internet (this was the fall of 2001), I spent hours and hours on the phone to cast a wide net and bring in 11 other people to participate in the first Master Class, which was slated for May 2002. It amused me that the 12th person to commit called me to sign on when I was at the airport picking Jeff up. It seemed that this was meant to be. What I didn't know at the time was that the New York City Master Classes would have a long—a very long—shelf life. To date, we've met 50-plus times!

But back to 2002—eek—now that I had gotten my wish, I would be hosting and participating in this amazing opportunity to learn from Jeff. The physical experiences of being overwhelmed and excited occurred simultaneously. Each of these feelings ratcheted up to a fever pitch, leaving me feeling like a balloon that was blown up and then released without being tied off.

I was to provide the physical space to meet (my home office) and, as is my wont (Jewish mother that I am), to furnish refreshments throughout the day. I figured that the protocol would be demanding and having fuel available between structures would be important. I also hoped that the atmosphere of my home would be quite different from the typical bridge-chairs-in-a-conference-room-under-fluorescent-lights setting typical of most workshops. And, in fact, beyond the magic that Jeff brought to the class, the cozy atmosphere did make the rigors of "performing" therapy in front of colleagues seem easier.

Additionally, as host (or, if you prefer, mother hen), I felt an obligation to check in throughout the time on how people were feeling given the intimidation that came with participating in this type of learning opportunity for the first time. What soon became clear was that it was, in part, the challenge that provoked the growth. And the growth may explain why the Master Classes soon took on a life of their own.

The organization of the Master Class involves each of us having a session with Jeff presenting a real issue. The Master Class felt like a safe space right from the start. During one of the first classes, a participant plopped down in the chair opposite Jeff and busted out with, "About this affair that I'm having…" And there have been many other disclosures along the way.

In addition to the sessions with Jeff, we work in groups of three. Each of us has a turn to be therapist for an attendee, patient to a different attendee, and supervisor of the therapist-patient dyad. Jeff then follows up by providing comprehensive supervision after each of these structures. At the end of each section, we make a bee-line for the food, the bathroom, and some schmoozing with classmates, who always become quick friends.

For me, there were at the start the custodial responsibilities of hosting and the terror of doing therapy "in public" for the first time. For Jeff there were two practical considerations: the cost of flying to New York and the cost of a hotel. To minimize Jeff's expenses, he stayed on the pullout couch in my office. I almost croaked when he accepted my offer. Now I was going to have a stranger on the other side of a door. Needless to say, all of this together allowed for very little sleep for four nights. And here I learned one important hypnotic factoid: how easy it is to go into trance when you are overwhelmed and exhausted.

What Happened Next

A few years ago Jeff invited me to take a role as adjunct instructor. It was an honor, of course. Now, more than participate, I would provide my own brand of supervision to each triad in addition to Jeff's. I knew that Jeff was doing for me what Milton Erickson had done for him. He was "dragging me up" with him.

By this time I had participated in many Master Classes, because they were held three or four times a year, and I had grown to enjoy my freedom to think outside the box and to really understand the benefit to the patient of using talk therapy as a launchpad for working experientially wherever possible. In some instances, "launchpad" was literal, since providing experiences by getting out of the chair is powerful stuff.

A new model developed: a Jeff-Helen team. Jeff continued to provide cognitive assessments of the therapist's work based not only on his skill as a therapist, but also on his encyclopedic knowledge of a host of approaches to therapy from many of the masters. My style was to select a small but noteworthy slice of the therapist's work and to experientially demonstrate the effectiveness of what he or she had accomplished, with the intent of integrating and enhancing self-esteem.

The combination of cognitive and experiential supervision has been very valuable to attendees. The breadth of Jeff's knowledge and his generosity in sharing it, and his encouragement of growth in us, remains core to the success and longevity of the Master Classes. And my burgeoning contribution was recently so generously articulated by a colleague: "I feel caught rather than taught."

This book is a testament to Jeff. It is an acknowledgment of Jeff's climb to his own great heights, his model of seeking excellence, and his gift to us of his embodiment of Milton Erickson's extraordinary work.

As Jeff likes to say, he's "lived with me" for almost a year, and I've seen him do in excess of 700 therapies. That's Jeff's count. My count is different. Within the first few Master Classes, I began to realize that Jeff had become my friend.

HELEN ADRIENNE, LCSW, BCD has been a psychotherapist in private practice in New York City since 1979. She is best known for providing mind/body and clinical hypnotherapy services to patients struggling with infertility, as well as teaching those techniques in her Two-Day Training Program and at national and international conferences. In 2002, Helen's invitation to Dr. Jeff Zeig to come to New York City to train colleagues marked the beginning of the now-popular New York City Master Classes. Her book, *On Fertile Ground: Healing Infertility*, launched as a #1 best seller on Amazon and is available there. www.helenadrienne.com.

Psychotherapist and writer **BARBARA BIRGE**, PhD, LPC, NCC, lives in Charlotte, NC, where she maintains a private practice. Former president of the North Carolina Society of Clinical Hypnosis and approved consultant of the American Society of Clinical Hypnosis, she received her doctorate in clinical psychology from Pacifica Graduate Institute with specialization in depth psychology. She served for six years on the North Carolina Humanities Council and has also served on the boards of Charlotte Friends of Jung and the Greater Carolinas Chapter of the American Red Cross, for which she is a disaster mental health volunteer.

Psychologist **GRETHE BRUUN**, cand. psych., graduated from University of Copenhagen, Denmark in 1981. She is a specialist and supervisor of psychotherapy and of child psychology engaged in supervision, coaching, hypnosis, and storytelling, and presides over master classes in supervision, supervisor education, and supervision groups with professionals. She is the author of two books on therapy and supervision, and has published articles on therapy, supervision, storytelling, hypnosis, and Footprintings. She leads workshops in Denmark, Germany, and on Faroe Islands, and has conducted workshops in Denmark with Rob McNeilly and Susan Dowell, as well as master classes with Jeff Zeig and James Warnke. grethe@psykologgruppen-naestved.dk

SUSAN DOWELL, LCSW, is a clinical social worker with a practice in New York City and Westchester. Hypnosis has been a very important part of her professional life and she has been teaching clinical hypnosis for over 20 years. After attending Jeff Zeig's first Master Class in New York, she became entranced with the Ericksonian model of treatment and Jeff's empowering way of teaching. She has attended almost all of his NYC classes. Susan has also developed a new Ego State treatment model called Footprintings, which is founded on many of the Ericksonian principles that she has come to appreciate. Susan is widowed, has two sons, and three most wonderful grandchildren.

CAROLINE CHINLUND, PhD, maintains a private practice in New York City with individuals of all ages, families, and couples. Her postgraduate training was at NYU, The Postgraduate Center for Mental Health, and NYSEPH. The New York seminar with Jeff Zieg has been a source of inspiration and growth for her as a person and a therapist for many years.

BETTE J. FREEDSON, LICSW, LCSW, CGP is a clinical social worker, Certified Group Psychotherapist, author, and speaker. Her specialties include stress management, skillful parenting, trauma recovery, and utilization of intuitive resources of the body/mind, including "soul wisdom." Bette is passionate about helping individuals develop strategies to enhance resilience and promote peace of mind. Trained in Ericksonian hypnosis, Bette conducts workshops that combine cognitive/behavioral coping strategies with guidance from the unconscious mind. Bette is the author of *Soul Mothers' Wisdom: Seven Insights for the Single Mother*, published by Pearlsong Press. She lives and practices in southern Maine. Bettefreedson.com

TOBI B. GODLFUS, LCSW-C, BCD is a clinical social worker in private practice in Germantown, MD. She is the author of *From Real Life to Cyberspace (and Back Again): Helping Our Young Clients Develop a Strong Inner Selfie*, published in 2017. She presents nationally and internationally on the importance of bringing the young client's digital life into therapy as an essential aspect of treatment. She has served on numerous faculties, including the American Association of Clinical Hypnosis (ASCH), the Society of Clinical and Experimental Hypnosis (SCEH), the European Society of Hypnosis (ESH), and the International Society of Hypnosis (ISH).

In addition to psychotherapy, **JULIE ANN HALL,** LCSW, has a background in art history and philosophy. She received her Masters in Social Work from NYU in 1986. In 1999, she completed her certification in hypnotherapy from NYSEPH. She has happily participated in many Master Classes with Jeff Zeig. In private practice, she specializes in long-term in-depth psychotherapy with individuals where she finds the use of hypnosis helpful. She also treats couples and families. In her free time Julie paints watercolors of ravens and flowers. She is grateful for the opportunities she has been given and the deep friendships she has.

WEI-KAI HUNG, EdM, graduated from Teachers College, Columbia University. He is a licensed mental health counselor in New York, and a licensed psychologist in Taiwan. He is past director of the counseling department of the Taiwan Institute of Psychotherapy and a frequent flyer at Dr. Zeig's New York Master Class (11 times and counting). He currently offers numerous trainings in Asia and in the US that integrate eastern approaches with Ericksonian Hypnosis. Wei-Kai serves as coordinator/assistant for Dr. Zeig's workshops in China, has translated and edited Dr. Zeig's book, *The Induction of Hypnosis*, into Chinese, and directed a 20-minute documentary film entitled "Jeffrey Zeig's Influence on Taiwan Psychotherapy."

CHARLES M. IKER, LCSW, has served as a clinical social worker since 1986, and has worked in a variety of venues, including residential treatment centers and hospitals, programs for children, addiction, and domestic violence. In private practice for some 20 years, he continues to study and train in the most current approaches to improve his clinical abilities, including clinical hypnosis, eye movement dissociation, reprocessing, and working with dissociation. He participated in a year-long training program with Bessel van der Kolk, MD, to learn his revolutionary approach to treating trauma, and most recently is exploring shorter term psychotherapies.

DANA LEBO, PhD, is a NC-licensed psychologist. She has lived on three continents, studied five languages, taught refugees in Egypt and the US, earned a PhD from Columbia University, and coached a soccer team of 11-year-old girls with a newborn in tow. She has published and presented internationally on women and work-life balance, counseled retired NFL players, and helped teenagers and older adults to write memoirs, among many other things. Dr. Lebo applies the lessons learned from her diverse experience and advanced studies in the brain, behavioral, and health sciences to her executive coach role at Bell Leadership Institute in Chapel Hill.

RICK MILLER, LICSW, psychotherapist and author, has served on the faculties of The International Society of Hypnosis, The Milton H. Erickson Foundation, The Brief Therapy Conference, The Society for Clinical and Experimental Hypnosis, The American Society of Clinical Hypnosis, The American Group Psychotherapy Association, The Couples Conference, and Harvard Medical School. The author of *Unwrapped: Integrative Therapy With Gay Men… The Gift of Presence* (2014) and *Mindfulness Tools for Gay Men in Therapy* (2016), he is also a contributor to *Psychology Today* with his blog *Unwrapped: Mind Body Wisdom and the Modern Gay Man*. His current project is a docuseries—GaySonsandMothers.com. www.rickmiller.biz

SARA MILLSTEIN, LCSW, PhD, is a psychotherapist in private practice in NYC. She writes: "My introduction to hypnosis was in an undergraduate psychology class. I suspect my reaction was similar to how patients sometimes react when I suggest hypnosis now: 'I can't be hypnotized.' 'I don't want to cluck like a chicken.' Years later, hypnosis is integral to my thinking about the people who come to my office for therapy. My patients have a wide array of symptoms, and regardless of whether or not I do a formal induction, my way of being with a patient is informed by all that I have learned studying Ericksonian Hypnosis."

SUSAN PINCO, PhD, LCSW is in private in NYC and teaches internationally, offering courses in powerful, somatically informed treatment modalities that bridge the gap between mind and body. Susan is an ASCH certified Hypnotherapist/Approved Consultant, an EMDR certified consultant, and a certified BrainSpotting (BSP) consultant and trainer. She offers courses in Crisis Communication and Crisis Response and the Mandala of Being, a Multi-Modal Approach to Spiritual and Psychological Practice. She is currently working on a book that encourages therapists to explore how they can utilize silence to facilitate integration and healing. www.coherentself.com

Rabbi **CHANOCH ROSENBERG** is the founder and director of From Problems to Solutions (FPTS), an institute in the greater New York area specializing in addressing personal, parenting, marital, and relationship challenges through facilitating goal oriented change. A noted consultant, speaker, and author, his works include *Shteig in Sheifos (Climbing Towards Aspirations)*, a bestselling Yiddish self-help/development book, as well as a relaxation/guided imagery book and audio CD, with a foreword by Jeffrey Zeig, PhD. Chanoch is passionate about empowering others to uncover their strengths, identify aspirations, embrace challenges, develop a healthy resilient mindset, and achieve meaningful transformative change.

CHRISTOPH SOLLMANN, Dr. phil., Dipl. Psych., a clinical and work psychologist, has maintained a private practice since 1989 (Germany), and is a coach and trainer in leadership and management skills. He is author of various books and articles focusing on management and hypnosis. He has received education in hypnotherapy at the Milton H. Erickson Foundation in Phoenix, Arizona and through attending the Master Classes in NYC with Jeffrey K. Zeig.

ROB STAFFIN, PsyD, ABPH is Vice President of the Clinical Hypnosis Society of NJ, an approved consultant for ASCH, and a diplomate of the American Board of Psychological Hypnosis, and teaches nationally and internationally. He says: "When I attended my first Master Class in 2002, I had no idea how much it would impact me personally or how profoundly it would impact my development as a clinician. I have gone spelunking in the lair of nagging concern; six-year-old Robbie Staffin has had an audience with the Dali Lama; and I have been literally reduced to sobs as I have felt the weight of compassion in the world."

Father **JAMES W. WARNKE**, MA, MSW, ACSW, LCSW recently retired from clinical practice after 36 years as a private practitioner in Teaneck, NJ. He served for many years on the faculty of the New York Milton H. Erickson Society for Psychotherapy and Hypnosis and on the faculty of the National Pediatric Hypnosis Training Institute (formally sponsored by the Society for Developmental Pediatrics). Jim is past president of the New York Milton H. Erickson Society for Psychotherapy and Hypnosis. Legally blind from birth, Jim continues to serve as an Episcopal Priest and he attends the NYC Master Class with Jeff Zeig twice yearly as he has since the first class.

JEFFREY K. ZEIG, PhD, is the Founder and Director of The Milton H. Erickson Foundation. Dr. Zeig is the architect of the Evolution of Psychotherapy Conference, Brief Therapy Conference, Couples Conference, and the International Congresses on Ericksonian Approaches to Hypnosis and Psychotherapy.

He is on the editorial board of numerous journals. He is also a Fellow of the American Psychological Association (Division 29, Psychotherapy, Division 30 Hypnosis) and the American Society of Clinical Hypnosis. Dr. Zeig is a Distinguished Practitioner in the National Academy of Practice in Psychology of the National Academies of Practice, and an Approved Supervisor of the American Association for Marriage and Family Therapy.

A clinical psychologist, he has a private practice and conducts workshops internationally in 40 countries and counting. He has been an invited speaker at major universities and teaching hospitals.

Jeffrey Zeig has edited, co-edited, authored, and coauthored 24 books on psychotherapy that appear in 15 languages.

www.ingramcontent.com/pod-product-compliance
Lightning Source LLC
Chambersburg PA
CBHW071641280326
41928CB00068B/2069